KNIGHT OF THE BURNING HEART

KNIGHT OF
THE BURNING HEART

The Story of John Wesley

By

LESLIE F. CHURCH, B.A., Ph.D.

*

ABINGDON–COKESBURY PRESS

New York · *Nashville*

TO YOUTH

IN WHOSE QUEST AND CONQUEST
I BELIEVE

CONTENTS

A LINCOLNSHIRE LAD

It was a queer old house in which John Wesley was born. Its timber and plaster walls had stood up bravely through many a storm, and once, a few months before little Jackie arrived, it was almost burnt down – some sparks were blown into its straw thatch, and the flames spread quickly. The rector, Samuel Wesley, had been visiting someone who was ill, at the other end of the village. 'As I was returning', he says, 'they brought me the news. I got a horse, rode up, and heard by the way that my wife, children, and books, were saved; for which God be praised, as well as for what He has taken.'

On June 28, 1703, little Jackie was born. The old rectory had been restored. It was built of timber and plaster, with a thatched roof, and seven main rooms, a kitchen, a hall, a parlour, and a buttery downstairs, and three large upper rooms besides the attics. There was a great barn, built of timber planks, and thatched, like the home, with straw, and most joyous of all, a dovecote, where even the children of Susanna learnt to play hide-and-seek.

In the little garden, with its wooden palings, at the south of the rectory, the eldest boy, Samuel, gathered round him his sisters, Emilia, Susanna, Mary, and

Mehetabel, and told them the great news. He was thirteen years old, and all his sisters were younger. Little Anne was only a baby still. They were happy children though they lived Spartan lives.

In this quaint old house little Jackie grew up. When he was two years old his father was arrested and taken to Lincoln Castle to be imprisoned as a debtor. Samuel Wesley was a loyal little man, very fond of his children, very clever and very conscientious, but he could never keep out of debt.

His wife, Susanna, was the daughter of the Rev. Dr. Annesley. Her sister, Judith, whose portrait was painted by Sir Peter Lely, was a famous beauty, but one who knew both the girls said, 'Beautiful as Miss Annesley appears, she was far from being as beautiful as Mrs. Wesley'.

Some people have thought she was harsh and did not understand the training of children. When we read of the rules and restrictions laid down for the family at Epworth we must judge them by the standards of the period. It is absurd to condemn Susanna, because she did not know the fuller and freer life of to-day.

In the seventeenth and eighteenth centuries education was at a low ebb. The record reveals conditions which were tragic. Rich children were spoilt. Their schooling was perfunctory and undisciplined. The peasants were for the most part illiterate, save in villages where Dames' schools afforded crude elementary teaching. The poor in the towns were chiefly concerned in securing a few pence from the labours of their children, who should have been at school.

Judging by the standards of to-day we should be shocked at many things that were commonplace when John Wesley was a child. Punishment was excessive and brutal. The public taste was not outraged by the sight of executions. In 1732, when William Hutton was ten years old, he watched the agonies of a woman fastened each day to the pillory and beaten through the streets with sadistic fury. One turns, with relief, from such a description to the comparatively gentle discipline of the Epworth rectory.

It is more accurate to say that Susanna Wesley was, in many ways, ahead of her time. As late as 1864, the following advertisement appeared in *The Times*: 'Boarding Schools Wanted, in London, for a boy nine years old, and two girls, six and seven years old, requiring firm discipline, having become wild and unruly, through neglect occasioned by family misfortunes. No holyday could be given, as holydays destroy any good effected at school.' It would have been more pleasant to sit with Sukey and Mehetabel, John and Charles in the Epworth schoolroom, than to have been the three little victims for sacrifice in 1864.

In the eighteenth century the Wesley household was a pattern. Judged by modern standards we should call the habits of the people filthy and their appetites bestial. They fed like animals and became gross in body, as contemporary pictures bear witness. It is against such a background that one must look at the clean, but sparsely furnished house at Epworth. In the big room where the children sat six hours a day, the mental discipline was certainly severe, but it was a splendid contrast to the coarse illiteracy of contemporary life. Before one condemns Susanna, or passes airy and superficial judgement on her work, we might well remember at least one of her results. In speaking of this period, Elizabeth Godfrey says, 'Wherever the preaching of John Wesley took root a Sunday School sprang up'. Those schools which taught general subjects as well as Scripture, were born in the Epworth rectory.

When one remembers that Rousseau would have disciplined a child who broke a window by forcing him to sit in the draught and catch cold, and that Mrs. Ruskin let John hold his finger against the hot bar of the grate to teach him not to play with fire – one questions whether Susanna Wesley was the harsh and soured martinet recent biographers have suggested.

It is true that to us, her rules and regulations seem a 'grisly code', but Walter de la Mare in considering it asks: 'Is it conceivable that any child thus brought up could come to a bad end? *Were* these children utterly cowed and suppressed, sucked dry of will and initiative? If their heredity is given its due weight a plain answer to this question at any rate will be found in the *Dictionary of National Biography*. Charles Wesley wrote over six thousand hymns; his brother John preached forty thousand sermons. That hardly suggests a lack of will or initiative.'

Both the grandfathers of the children in the Epworth rectory had been clergymen of the Church of England, and had forfeited their churches because they refused to accept the 'Act of Uniformity'. Susanna was determined that her children should be strong enough to obey the voice of conscience at all costs. They were happy enough, in spite of all the discipline. Indeed, according to Dr. Adam Clarke, 'There were few misunderstandings amongst them, and no unbrotherly or vindictive passions: and they had the common fame of being the most loving family in the County of Lincoln'.

Every day they came in to dinner and sat at a little table, with their chairs close to their father and mother. They were allowed to eat as much as they would, but not to call for anything. They had to whisper respectfully to the maid who came and told Susanna. The servants were forbidden to do anything for the children unless they were asked politely. No orders were given by the children. When they were old enough to use a knife and fork properly they came to the big table. Their mother says, 'Morning they always had spoon-meat; sometimes at night. But whatever they had, they were never permitted at those meals to eat of more than one thing, and of that sparingly enough. Drinking or eating between meals was never allowed unless in case of sickness, which seldom happened'.

It was rather a severe life for a little boy, but it helped to make Jackie a strong man. He learnt to say the Lord's Prayer in the morning and at bed-time, and as he grew older a little prayer for his parents was added. Family prayers were taken morning and evening. One can picture the seven little children of whom Jackie, or John Benjamin – to give him his proper name – was the youngest, sitting solemnly, listening to their father as he read the portion for the day.

The night before his sixth birthday, Jackie wondered what all the commotion was about. The house was set specially in order because another child was going to begin his schooling. It was a rule in the Epworth rectory that none of the children should learn to read until they were five. There is rather an interesting reason for that. Samuel was the eldest child, and he did not learn to speak until he was nearly five years old. He used to wander about the rooms of the rambling old house, carrying under his arm a favourite cat, and sometimes hiding away with it. One day he could not be found anywhere. His mother went through all the rooms, calling his name. Presently she heard a voice from under the table, 'Here I am, mother', and looking down, to her surprise, she saw Sammy sitting comfortably there with his cat. That was the first occasion on which any one had heard him speak. After that she taught him to read. Probably that is why she fixed that age for all the other children to begin to go to school.

The school itself was held in the rectory, and Mrs. Susanna Wesley was the teacher. First of all she taught the new child the letters of the alphabet – just one day was allowed for that. Afterwards he began to read, and each one began with the first chapter of Genesis. One can picture little Jackie, just after his sixth birthday, sitting solemnly on one of those special little chairs, trying to spell out the first verse of the first chapter of the first book in the Bible. That is really a landmark – 'In the beginning God created the heaven and the earth'. This was the first lesson he learnt in his mother's school, and all his life he was developing it.

It was not much wonder that John Wesley became known as a Methodist for as a little boy he learnt to do everything methodically. It seemed that the whole house at Epworth was governed by rule. Each day in the week Susanna had a special talk with one of her children. On Monday with Mollie, on Tuesday with Hettie, on Wednesday with Nancy, on Thursday with Jackie, on Friday with Patty, on Saturday with Charles, and with Emilia and Sukey on

Sunday. It all sounds very stilted to us, but it worked out very well. Twenty years after he had left home John Wesley wrote to his mother, 'If you can spare me only that part of Thursday evening which you formerly bestowed on me in another manner I doubt not it would be as useful now for correcting my heart as it was in forming my judgement'. Perhaps it is because of what she learnt on those Fridays that Patty or Martha grew up with an amazingly generous heart, so that her brother Charles once said, 'It is in vain to give Pat anything for she always gives it away to some people poorer than herself'.

Though there were so many rules, and so much strictness, Susanna was only anxious to teach the children to think for themselves. She wrote to Sukey in 1710, 'The main thing which is now to be done is, to lay a good foundation, that you may act upon *principles*, and be always able to satisfy yourself, and give a good reason to others of the Faith that is in you – for any one who makes a profession of religion, only because it is the custom of the country in which they live or because their parents do so . . . will never be able to stand in the day of temptation'.

About eight months after he started school there was a sudden interruption. Everybody had gone to bed and the whole family were sound asleep at midnight. Suddenly old Samuel woke up with a start – some one was crying 'Fire! fire!' He leaped out of bed and rushed to the door to find the whole house full of smoke. Once again the thatched roof was burning, and was about to fall in. Quickly he wakened his wife and two of the girls. Susanna rushed to the door of the nursery where a maid was sleeping with the three other little girls and John, and Charles who was not quite two months old. The nurse leaped out of bed, taking little Charles in her arms and called to the others to follow. Three sisters ran out through the door and down through the smoke to the hall but little Jackie slept on.

Some got out through the windows, others by the garden door, and Mrs. Wesley, thinking all were safe, waded through the sea of fire to the safety of the open air. Outside the family was gathered together. Suddenly they realized that one was missing. Above the roar of the flames they thought they heard a little voice cry out. Old Samuel turned and made for the house. He tried to climb up the flaming staircase but it crashed beneath his feet. There was no way to that upper floor. He fell on his knees and besought God to save his child.

Upstairs little Jackie rubbed his eyes – they were smarting with the smoke, and the room was very bright. For a moment he thought morning had come. He peeped between the curtains about the window, and saw nothing but flames. He ran to the door and opened it. There was no way through which he could pass. At last he climbed up to the window-ledge, and suddenly the crowd saw him.

There was no time to fetch a ladder – one of the villagers bent his back against the wall, another climbed up and clutched the ledge. With a struggle he managed to catch the little fellow as he knelt on the window-sill, and brought him down, safe and sound, just as the roof fell in.

Nobody knows the name of that man, but he gave a great gift to the world that night. When Jackie was grown to be a man he looked back and remembered, and saw himself, 'a brand plucked from the burning!'

The east wind was blowing hard against the burning wood, there was little left of the rectory, but outside there, on the grass lawn, the rector knelt down with the crowd, and gave God thanks. 'Come, neighbours', said he, 'let us kneel down, let us give thanks to God, He has given me all my eight children; let the house go, I am rich enough.'

So, in mid-winter, on February 9, 1709, Samuel Wesley found himself and his family without a roof to cover their heads. Friends took them in, and indeed they were not much poorer now than they had been before, except for one thing – they had lost confidence in their neighbours. The rector felt there was treachery in the air. Some of the people, he felt sure, had set the rectory on fire. The country round Epworth is called the Isle of Axholme. It was encircled by rivers and was neither fen nor marsh. Constant floods made farming difficult and uncertain. The people were irritable and hard pressed.

They did not like the rector's politics, and they detested his sermons which reproved them for their violence and ill-temper.

Once some of them gathered round the old rectory and kept up a hideous din all night long, banging tin cans, and letting off guns. A little while after, three of Samuel's cows were wounded, and his favourite dog was deliberately hurt. Evidently the fire was the work of these people but the rector did not give in. Putting his family in the homes of different friendly neighbours, he set to work to build his house again. The day after the fire he was poking about amongst the ashes and found two small pieces of paper, partly burnt. One of them was a leaf from his Bible, and on it he read, in Latin, 'Sell all that thou hast, take up thy cross and follow Me'. The other had one of his hymns on it:

> Behold the Saviour of mankind
> Nailed to the shameful tree!
> How vast the love that Him inclined
> To bleed and die for me!

The old man thanked God once again and took courage.

For a few months the children lived in other people's houses, and their mother lost control of them. As soon as the new rectory was ready they came back, and immediately they settled down to live 'by rule' again.

So the days went on, and little Jackie grew brave and strong. His mother struggled grimly to feed and clothe her big family. Upstairs, in the back room which was his study, the old rector wrote hour after hour – always busy on what he dreamed would be his masterpiece. Often Hettie would sit on the back stairs to guard her father from interruptions. While the poet fought out 'The Battle of Blenheim' in ungainly metre, Jackie would steal past on tiptoe, hand in hand with Charles, the poet to be.

Meanwhile he had his own little battles to face. When he was eight years old he got small-pox. His father was away at the time, but Susanna wrote to him cheerfully and not a little proudly, 'Jack has borne his disease bravely, like a man, and indeed, like a Christian, without complaint, though he seemed angry at the small-pox when they were sore, as we guessed by his looking sourly at them, for he never said anything'. That was the beginning of the courage which the Knight of the Burning Heart showed later when he faced fierce mobs or storms at sea, or the wilder storms within his own heart.

It was when he was eight years old that his father first allowed him to take the Sacrament of Holy Communion. This meant a great deal to him, for he had been instructed by Susanna and realized something of what it meant.

For five years John Wesley was taught by his mother in the little school within their home. Every day in the big room, the children worked from nine till twelve, and from two till five. They were never allowed to play in the street or to run wild. The rector grew flax and interested himself in the farming life of the people round about, and the children romped in the fields with the dogs and cattle.

CHAPTER 2

A GOWN-BOY
AT CHARTERHOUSE

SUDDENLY there dawned a wonderful day for Jackie. He was to go to school in London. In January 1714, the family heard that the Duke of Buckingham had nominated him to Charterhouse. It seemed a far cry from the rectory in the sombre Isle of Axholme to the heart of the city, and the discipline of a famous school. The boy was excited and eager; his mother was anxious but resigned. How could she close the door that had opened! The time was coming when the training of the schoolroom at Epworth was to be tested in the rough and tumble outside. She waved farewell, and went back again to pray and to teach.

It was all very exciting. The little boy just over ten years old, rode up to London to mix for the first time in his life with the great world. How strange he felt amongst that crowd of boys! There were forty-four in his house, gown-boys, and they had not learnt politeness in a rectory schoolroom! How prim and proper he must have seemed to them!

There he is sitting in chapel, dressed in his little black cloth gown and knee-breeches, perched somewhere in one of those rows of seats which were placed solemnly in front of the Founder's tomb. The great Head Master, Dr. Thomas Walker, very near him, in a strangely erected seat, must have looked very formidable to a little boy. He was not a new head master! He had been there thirty-five years. People like Addison and Steele had been amongst the boys whom he taught. In another seat, rather like a pepper-box, sat the Usher or Second Master, Andrew Tooke. A little further off, but very important, sat the organist, T. Love. Amongst all these great people in the somewhat dim light, the little boy from the Epworth rectory looked round, gazed at the tomb of Thomas Sutton, Esq., looked out of the corner of his eyes at Dr. Walker, and wondered what his sisters Emilia, Hettie, and the rest were doing in that school that was so different, in the little room at Epworth.

It was certainly a sudden change for him. Food had never been varied, or too plentiful at Epworth, but each child had had enough. At Charterhouse the big boys organized raids on the meat supply of the little boys. The probability is that he did not have much meat there at all but lived even more plainly than at Epworth. However, he was not the kind of boy to grumble – every morning he ran three times round the Green – a distance of a mile – and so was always 'in training'.

Round and round the field ran the little fellow who was some day to be a leader of men. The very ground

23

on which he trod was an epitome of history. Nearly four hundred years before it had been called No Man's Land. Then came a great pestilence to London, and fifty thousand dead were buried there. In Pardon Churchyard and New Church Haw, they lay, victims of the Plague. Presently the monks came – twenty-four Carthusians – and sang their orisons in a new Priory built to receive them. They did not stay long. A day came when the monasteries were destroyed, and the monks fled, or, dallying, were hanged at Tyburn. Court officials dwelt in the new mansion, and the young Queen Elizabeth was the guest of Lord North whilst they prepared for her coronation. From Charterhouse, Thomas Howard, Duke of Norfolk, went to die the death of a traitor, because someone had poked out his secret papers hidden under the tiles. At last, a wealthy merchant, Thomas Sutton, dreamed a dream of a hospital for aged men and a school for poor boys. On June 22, 1611, he obtained Letters Patent from King James, and his dream became reality.

A hundred years later little Jackie Wesley galloped round the Green, or sat solemnly reading the classics where wretched, plague-stricken bodies had found resting-place at last, where Kings and Queens had paused at the foot of their thrones, where traitors had bidden farewell to life itself and where a successful merchant had found his greatest joy. Nobody noticed the frail little figure sitting amongst the rest.

He was not brilliant enough to attract attention by his genius, nor was he dull enough to be accused of indolence. The Governors were important men. They were heirs of a great tradition. Archbishops and Lord Chief Justices were their predecessors. Oliver Cromwell and Judge Jeffreys had been on the Board. How could their pompous successors be expected to notice the coming of a small boy from a poverty-stricken Lincolnshire parsonage?

They passed him in the cloisters as unnoticed as the other ghosts of Charterhouse. The little boy stole by in the shadows unconscious that long after-wards those walls would ring with his name as generation after generation of Carthusians sang their school song –

> Wesley, John Wesley, was one of our company,
> Prophet untiring and fearless of tongue;
>   Down the long years he went,
>   Spending, yet never spent,
> Serving his God with a heart ever young.

He was only at the beginning of his journey, but he began well. Modest and industrious, accepting hardship without complaint, he loved Charterhouse, in spite of its ghosts and its bullies, and within its walls learnt to be a man.

When he had been at school about two years strange things began to happen in the old Epworth rectory. Loud knockings were heard about the house, and no one could tell who made them. When the children ran from one room to another, peering into every corner, there was nobody there. It must be a ghost! They were not very frightened. It was rather good fun. They named him 'Old Jeffrey'. He was specially annoying during family prayers, and most particularly when Samuel Wesley prayed for the King! The family thought he *must* be a Jacobite. Doors were banged open, little soft taps were heard on the wall, the cradle began to rock, stones seemed to be thrown amongst the bottles that lay under the stairs. The big dog, a mastiff, began to cry and whine. Even Susanna wondered. Once she saw something like a badger running out of the room. For more than two months there was constant excitement but no one seems to have been very much afraid.

When Jackie grew up he examined all the evidence and came to the conclusion that it really was a ghost. Many people think it is much more likely that it was some of the villagers, who were still angry with the rector, and often tried to irritate him and perhaps hoped, eventually, to drive him away.

I think I can see little Jackie, walking down the cloisters at Charterhouse, whispering the exciting story of Old Jeffrey to some of his friends. He would feel rather important – a boy with a ghost of his own!

In spite of scanty meals, and perhaps a little bully-ing, and quite a lot of hard work, Jack learnt to love

Charterhouse. He little thought that some day he would be called 'the greatest Carthusian'. He was just a little boy who had learnt his lessons pretty well, grown strong and wiry although he was still rather small. But when he left Charterhouse in 1720 he set out for Christ Church, Oxford with a School Exhibition of £40 a year. The masters thought he was a 'very promising classic' and that he had a special gift for Latin verse.

Before he went to the University his father had asked him to call and see Dr. Sacheverell, hoping that he would give him letters of recommendation to Oxford.

It was an exciting journey, as a journey always has been to the schoolboy just leaving school. The rector of St. Andrew's, Holborn, was a great man now. A few years before Dr. Sacheverell had preached a sermon which annoyed the Whigs. He had been impeached in the House of Lords and suspended, but what did that matter? The Tories had come back to power and he was in favour again.

The Charterhouse boy left the quiet cloisters, crossed the Green, and came out through the great gate on his way to Cheapside. Through narrow little streets, with posts to mark out the paths for pedestrians, he walked eagerly. Wooden stalls stood in the gutters, porters swung along carrying sedan-chairs with great ladies going to the rout; now and then a coach rumbled past. Everybody was shouting or ringing bells. The shop-signs creaked on their rusty hinges, and the street-sellers cried their goods. 'A Bed Matt or a Door Matt', 'Any Bakeing Peares', 'Buy a Rabbet a Rabbet', 'Buy my Four Ropes of Hard Onyons', 'Delicate Cucumbers to Pickle', 'Old Chaires to Mend', 'Old Satten, Old Taffety or Velvet', 'Hott Baked Wardens Hott' – surely you could buy all the treasures in the world between Charterhouse and Holborn. The small boy lingered a little to catch the fragrance of the hot pies and wished his father were a great gentleman whose son could buy a savoury pie, but the man with the steaming tray passed on. 'Hott Baked Wardens Hott', be sang, and the boy sighed.

Up the street he trudged. There were so many queer signs outside the taverns – Blue Boars, and Red Lions, Flying Pigs, and Hogs in Armour – surely there could not be all these wonderful creatures in the world – unless in Africa!

How could one hurry with so many brave sights! The bishop drove past, with his lackey bewigged. Gentlemen of quality walked on their way to the chocolate-houses, to sip and to chatter politics or scandal. How elegantly they tapped their snuff-boxes! Brave world of colour and fashion. Dull little gown-boy of Charterhouse.

Soldiers pass; the scarlet and blue of the Life Guards, the long red coats of the Halberdiers – the heart of the boy beats quickly. There is something in him that responds to the quick march of this world of which he has known so little.

Some one sticks up a play-bill. He stops, as any boy would, to read. It tells of a new paradise at Hampstead: 'These are to give notice that Belsize [a stately building in front of the highway of Hampstead] is now opened for the whole season, and that all things are most commodiously concerted for the reception of gentlemen and ladies; the park, wilderness and gardens being wonderfully improved, and filled with a variety of birds, which compose a most melodious and delightsome harmony. Every morning, at seven o'clock, the music begins to play, and continues the whole day through; and any persons inclined to walk and divert themselves in the morning, may as cheaply breakfast there, on tea and coffee, as in their own chambers. . . .' What passionate dreams of delight! What cared the little gown-boy that Hampstead was a long way out, that highwaymen and footpads lurked by the road! He would not hide behind the 'twelve stout fellows completely armed' who, the bill said, would protect travellers to Belsize.

Eh! dear! So this is Holborn, and here is the house of the reverend Dr. Sacheverell. He must pull himself together. His father had told him the great man would open the gates of Oxford for him. Oxford! Epworth! Oxford – Dr. Sacheverell!

But John Wesley was not very much impressed.

This is what he says: 'I was a very little fellow when I was introduced to him. I found him alone, as tall as a maypole, and as fine as an archbishop. After I made known to him the object of my visit, he said, "You are too young to go to the University, you cannot know Greek and Latin yet, go back to school".' This might have rebuffed a boy who had not grown accustomed to meet criticism. He said: 'I looked at him as David looked at Goliath and despised him in my heart. I thought, if I do not know Greek and Latin better than you I ought to go back to school indeed. I left him, and neither entreaties nor commands could have again brought me back to him.'

He had no letter in his pocket, but he does not seem to have been distressed. He was going to Oxford and if Dr. Sacheverell would not open the door, he was prepared to climb over the top.

CHAPTER 3

CITY OF DREAMING SPIRES

When gown-boys left Charterhouse they received £100 if they decided to go into business, but if they went to the University they were given £40 a year for three years, and £100 for the fourth year. There was no hesitation as to which of the two courses young Jack Wesley should take, and so he was entered at Christ Church, Oxford, on June 24, 1720.

He was seventeen, the age of dreams, and the coach was carrying him to Oxford, a city of dreams. The horses galloped down the High Street to the old Mitre Inn; he had arrived at a new beginning. The road was still paved with cobble-stones, heaps of rubbish lay round about, but the boy, with perhaps the sharpest eyes in the world, looked down the street, and saw the dreaming spires and the challenging towers of Oxford. He was a lucky fellow. His father had been a student at Exeter College, very poor but very happy. His brother Samuel was also an Oxford man. That night, when he settled down, feeling a little lonely in his room at Christ Church, his dream, of what might be, mounted up to the heavens like the spires and the towers about him.

He decided to keep a diary, and its rather browned pages still tell us of his life as an undergraduate. The little book, with its marble-cardboard cover, is a revelation of his life from the age of seventeen to twenty-two.

It was not very easy for him to live on the little money he had. His father and mother made heroic efforts to send him some from time to time, but there were all sorts of expenses – shoe-leather, sugar for his tea, and the hire of a horse to go and see his friends, the Kirkhams, over the Cotswolds. There was the expense of paying for a window he had broken, the need for money to buy books and to ensure a very meagre allowance for clothes. All these things threatened to force him into debt. As he struggled to make both ends meet his mother tried to help him, 'Dear Jack, Be not discouraged; do your duty; keep close to your studies, and hope for better days. Perhaps, notwithstanding all, we shall pick up a few crumbs for you before the end of the year. Dear Jackie, I beseech Almighty God to bless you'. They were struggling against a bad harvest, a reduced income and the ravages of small-pox in the rectory at Epworth.

Meanwhile Jackie kept them posted with the news. 'We are most of us now very healthy at Oxford, which may be in some measure owing to the frosty weather we have had lately. Fruit is so very cheap that apples may be had almost for fetching; and other things are both plentiful and good. We have indeed, something bad as well as good, for a great many rogues are about the town, in so much that it is exceedingly unsafe to be out late at night. . . . The chief piece of news with us is concerning the famous Jack Sheppard's escape from Newgate, which is indeed as surprising as most stories I have heard.' The rest of the letter tells about his reading a book on health which prescribes a special diet for students, about his having a bad cut on his thumb which was now nearly cured, about his writing to his sisters, and his desire for news from Epworth. The letter ends, 'The scantiness of my paper obliges me to conclude with begging yours and my father's blessing on your dutiful son, John Wesley'.

For five years the undergraduate worked very hard eking out his scanty allowance as best he could. His mother wrote to him, 'I wish you would save all the money you can conveniently spare, not to spend on a visit, but for a wiser and better purpose – to pay debts, and make yourself easy'.

In the rectory, though there was never any money to spare, Samuel Wesley, proud of his boys at Oxford, struggled to send them a little money now and then. 'Since you have now for some time bit upon the bridle', he writes, 'I will take care hereafter to put a little honey upon it, as oft as I am able; but then it shall be of my own mere motion, as the last five pounds was, for I will bear no rival in my kingdom. Your affectionate father, Samuel Wesley.'

Meanwhile John was quite natural in his social

relationships. He had a few friends but he did not waste time with mere acquaintances. The Knight was on his quest. He scarcely knew what he was seeking, but he struggled towards a dim goal, and the first thing was to fit his mind for the journey. He rode a little and walked a good deal, played tennis and other games, but the question of money was always worrying him. There were hundreds of other students at Oxford and most of them were well-to-do. They dressed smartly and drank deeply, but John Wesley struggled on, and tried to pay his way. His mother wrote asking him to go to the barber and have his hair cut because she thought it would improve his health! He was determined, as he wrote, that unless his health was really bad he would not spend two or three pounds a year on the barber. Behind him there always seemed to be this spectre of poverty.

Life at the University was notoriously shallow. Students who studied were in the minority. Degrees were given almost solely for residence. Only the determined few attained that culture which is the reward of self-discipline and ordered thought.

John was very dissatisfied with himself during the first few years. He still said his prayers and read his Bible, but he was uneasy. Something was missing. He had no joyous sense of pleasing God. Things that other people would not have noticed seemed to make a deep impression on him. One night, for instance, when he was feeling particularly happy the old porter came to his rooms to speak to him. 'Go home and get another coat,' said John, as he looked at the old one the man was wearing. 'This is the only coat I have in the world and I thank God for it,' said the man. 'Go home and get your supper then,' said Wesley. 'I've had nothing to-day but a drink of water, and I thank God for that,' the man replied. 'It is late,' said Wesley, 'and you'll be locked out, then what will you have to thank God for?' 'I will thank Him that I have the dry stones to lie on,' said the porter. 'John,' said Wesley, 'you thank God when you have nothing to wear, nothing to eat, no bed to lie upon; what else do you thank Him for?' 'Well,' said the porter, 'I thank Him that He has given me my life and being, a heart to love Him, and a desire to serve Him.' The smile faded from Wesley's face – it was not a joke any more. Somewhere in the man's heart was something that he himself did not possess. He wondered what it was; he longed to find out. The Knight was beginning his quest.

In 1725 he read two books, one by Thomas à Kempis called *The Imitation of Christ*, the other by Jeremy Taylor, called *Holy Living and Holy Dying*. These books made a great impression on him. He did not agree with them. No undergraduate agrees with any book! But he wrote home to his mother, Susanna, and asked her what she thought about his problem.

She answered him at length. It was not a very good answer really, and he was not satisfied.

About the beginning of the year, after he had been four years at Christ Church, he wrote to his parents and told them that he wanted to become a Christian minister. They were surprised, but after three weeks his father wrote, giving him his blessing. In due course he was ordained a deacon by Bishop Potter. The entry in his little diary reads, 'On September 19, 1725, I was ordained Deacon by the Bishop of Oxford. Afternoon: Walked in Trinity Gardens....'

He preached his first sermon at South Leigh, a little village near Witney, in January 1726. Two months later his father was delighted because he was elected Fellow of Lincoln College. The old man had scarcely a penny left, but what did money matter? He wrote, 'What will be my fate, God only knows. Wherever I am, my Jack is Fellow of Lincoln'. The fact that he had this Fellowship meant that John would receive a sum of money each year which lightened one of his burdens considerably.

He was now working very hard. 'Leisure and I have parted company', he said. It was a final farewell for one can never imagine him at leisure again. He was made Greek Lecturer and Moderator of the Classics, which meant that he presided at the debates which were held every day in Lincoln College.

When Samuel, his elder brother, came up to visit

John and Charles, who was now at Oxford too, he
was evidently anxious for he wrote a poem:

> One or two questions more before I end,
> That doth much concern a brother and a friend,
> Does John seem bent beyond his strength to go,
> To his frail carcass literally so?
> Lavish of health, as if in haste to die,
> And shorten time, to ensure Eternity?

CHAPTER 4

STRANGE INTERLUDE

THE next ten years of John Wesley's life were a strange mixture of romance, drudgery and stern self-discipline. In his quest he passed from the joyous circle of friends in Stanton Harcourt through the dismal servitude of Wroote, to the stress and strain of the Holy Club at Oxford. It was an amazing pilgrimage.

On an early spring day in 1725 two young men rode out from Oxford on their way to a rectory, set in a beautiful village, thirty-six miles away. The rector's son, Robert Kirkham, was rather proud of his friend, and John Wesley, perhaps a little timidly, valued his friendship for his own sake but even more, for the sake of his family.

The merry circle of the Kirkhams was a welcome change from the remorseless studies at Oxford. No wonder that the vivacity of Sally, and the daring ridicule of Betty – Bob's two sisters – shook the young don out of his natural solemnity. There were days of happy wandering over the Cotswolds, days of pleasant dalliance on the terrace at Stanton, days when the grim struggle to attain seemed unreal, almost unnecessary. It was not that John lost his sense of values, but that suddenly he entered a new, care-free company of normal people who were willing to be interested in the things that were dearest to him. It was Sally who introduced him to a book which made a deep impression on him, *The Imitation of Christ*, by Thomas à Kempis. They discussed it together, for Sally was something of a theologian, but she was also a woman with bright eyes and a ready wit. Whilst Betty was amused at his solemnity, Sally had a mood which accepted it.

Recent research by Mrs. Elsie Harrison, seems to prove conclusively that it was Sally and not Betty who won Wesley's heart. It was an idyllic friendship which, for a moment, seemed as though it would become more intimate.

There were others who visited the rectory at Stanton, and formed a little circle. From the neighbouring village of Buckland came Anne Granville and Mary, her sister, already a widow. They were descendants of the famous Sir Richard Grenville, and were 'ladies of quality'. How could the young Oxford tutor withstand the charm of Mrs. Pendarves, whom Edmund Burke described as 'the model of a perfect fine woman', and whom all her friends had pitied when at the age of eighteen she had been married to a dissolute and gouty husband! Now she was a young widow, brilliant rather than tragic, polished and well-versed in a wisdom of which Wesley knew nothing.

It was a new world to him and he enjoyed it.

The friends wrote to each other constantly, following the fashion of the day in using nicknames with a romantic and semi-classical sound. Sally was Sappho and sometimes Varanese, Mary Pendarves was Aspasia, John Wesley was Cyrus, and Charles when, later, he joined the group was Araspes. The correspondence was interesting but to a modern reader would seem utterly unreal and artificial.

How deeply John Wesley was affected by Varanese it is difficult to judge. Certainly he admired her and rejoiced in her friendship. Whether he would like to have married her is a moot point. She settled the question, if question there were, by marrying the village schoolmaster, John Chapone. Recent writers have suggested that John Wesley was heart-broken, and that all the rest of his life, he was influenced by this disappointment. That is a purely speculative conclusion. It is certain that his friendship with Varanese and with Aspasia was a treasured memory. It is equally certain that it was an education. There is no evidence to suggest that the marriage of either of these ladies had any tragic significance for John Wesley. His association with them was an innocent and beneficial experience, but it was neither a life-long obsession nor the occasion of an act of desperate renunciation.

They were happy days, these, in the Cotswolds. Perhaps they tided him over the period of stark struggle through which he had to pass. No one who appreciates the value of evidence could describe them in the language of vulgar intrigue or amorous adventure.

In August 1727, he left Oxford to help his father who was sixty-five and in indifferent health. In addition to Epworth, Samuel Wesley was responsible for the neighbouring parish of Wroote, and his son now relieved him of this charge.

It was a sudden change from the comparative comfort of his rooms at Lincoln College to the dismal house in the little village in the Isle of Axholme. 'It was a poor place surrounded with bogs,' he said. The old parsonage was 'roofed with thatch and made lively by the mingled music of kittens and whelps, pigs and porkets, bellowing kine and bleating lambs, quacking ducks and fluttering hens'. For a great part of the year it was isolated by flood-water, and the parishioners were compelled to journey by boat.

It is a dreary picture of village life, but it is only fair to compare it with eighteenth-century conditions in Europe at large. The peasant on the continent fared worse than his English neighbour. He was little better than a serf still. The princelings looked upon their subjects as useful for beaters in the hunting season, for lackeys in their stables and palaces, or for soldiers in the ambitious games of statecraft. They sometimes as Thackeray said 'swapped a battalion to buy a necklace for a pretty dancer'.

Whilst the villagers were ignorant and crude in

their habits, they were free to choose their occupations and to win a livelihood from the soil. Life was hard enough, and their outlook was limited, but the squire was little better off. He lived in his uncomfortable mansion, with little thought of occupying his mind with anything beyond fox-hunting, visits to the tavern, and a certain set attitude towards all innovation. He made, once in a while, a journey to town. His portrait was painted in coat and waistcoat which his father had worn before him, and as he adopted his father's clothes so he held tenaciously to his father's politics. The portrait in the *Tatler* describes him, mounted on a stout cob, followed by his favourite spaniel – 'a good dog, sir – always bites Dissenters'. 'Weather, sir, what weather we've had since the Whigs came into power!' Dear old Tory, fox-hunting squire, growing up on his little patch of ground with the vegetables, and like them rotting in decay on the same little patch. He knew no better, nor was he likely to learn until a prophet arose in the land. Sunday by Sunday he slept peacefully in his great square pew, while the parson droned his platitudes.

If the squire was dull the rest of the parishioners were duller. In Wroote, according to Hettie Wesley, 'the people were unpolished wights, their heads as impervious as stones'. They needed a message which would reach their hearts. For more than two years John Wesley remained amongst them. He does not seem to have had much success in his ministry. He himself wrote of it, 'I preached much, but saw no fruit of my labour. Indeed, it could not be that I should; for I neither laid the foundation of repentance, nor of believing the gospel'. Week after week he preached in the little brick church, but his sermons did not do much to change the people of Wroote. There was something obviously missing. He was discouraged and uneasy. Clouds were gathering at Epworth, where his sister had met with misfortune. There seemed no clear call to him. He buried himself in his books.

Once he considered the prospect of securing a post as schoolmaster in Yorkshire, hoping that he might live in seclusion and continue his study of the mystics. His mother strongly opposed the suggestion, but it was not Susanna who finally dissuaded him. In the North he met 'a serious man' whose advice made a permanent impression upon him. 'Sir,' said he, 'you wish to serve God and go to heaven; remember you cannot serve Him alone; you must, therefore, find companions or make them; the Bible knows nothing of solitary religion.' It was a severe rebuff to the curate of Wroote. Once more it was unpleasantly plain that he was lacking in the qualities of a Christian minister. Canon Overton describes him as being at this time 'simply a high-and-dry Churchman of the old school'.

In 1728 he had been ordained priest by Bishop

Potter at Oxford, but had returned again to Wroote where he remained till November 1729. A letter from Dr. Morley, Rector of Lincoln College, recalled him to take up his duties as a junior Fellow again. He left the pitiful little parish, where he had failed so lamentably, and came back to Oxford to find that something had happened which vitally affected im.

His brother Charles, four years younger than John, had gone to Westminster School at the age of eight. Fortunately brother Samuel was a master there, and more fortunate still, he had married the daughter of the Rev. John Berry who kept a house for boarders at Westminster. When he was fourteen Charles was elected a King's Scholar, and four years later became Captain of the school.

We can catch a glimpse or two of him through the years. Every morning he rises at a quarter past five, washes in the cloisters, joins in the Latin prayers, and proceeds to 'do his Latin grammar' till breakfast-time, at eight o'clock. Lessons continue till noon; then comes dinner. Two hours more of lessons are followed by a short interval, then still more lessons till supper, and at eight o'clock he goes to bed. Monitors take care that he speaks Latin all the time. It is not an easy day; even the rigours of the school at the Epworth rectory seem less demanding.

Once he had a never-to-be-forgotten fight. Little James Murray was surrounded by a crowd of bigger boys. 'Jacobite! Jacobite!' they shouted as they pounded him with their fists. A trim figure burst through the ring, smiting right and left. The suddenness of the onslaught scattered the bullies and young Murray was rescued. Long years afterwards two old men met – Charles Wesley and James Murray who had become the famous Lord Mansfield. They remembered the hour of deliverance and chuckled.

Just before he left Westminster, Charles had to make a momentous decision. A distant relative, Garrett Wesley, had written from Ireland to the Rector of Epworth offering to adopt Charles and make him his heir. The youth wrote to his father for advice, but old Samuel sturdily refused to make the decision. So many writers have caricatured the Rector of Epworth, conveniently ignoring this and many another evidence of his good qualities. The 'Quilp-like figure' they have described would hardly have missed such an opportunity! It would have meant one less child to feed and a little more money for Samuel, 'the spendthrift'. Such a picture does not fit this incident. Besides, something made Charles, himself, refuse the tempting offer. What was it? If it was, as seems most likely, the fact that he did not want to be separated from his family, it is a further criticism of recent pictures of the stern, almost inhuman relationships which are alleged to have existed in the Wesley family. Charles refused the fortune, preferring to remain the penniless son of a poverty-stricken country parson and his patient, strong-willed wife.

In 1726 he went up, with a scholarship, to Christ Church, Oxford. He was a bonny lad, not very tall but handsome enough. Almost immediately he was surrounded by friends. He was merry and enthusiastic. Life at Oxford, or indeed life anywhere, attracted him. One of his contemporaries, John Gambold, said, 'He was a man made for friendship, who by his cheerfulness and vivacity would refresh his friend's heart, with attentive consideration, would enter into and better all his concerns; so far as he was able would do everything for him, great or small'. What a success he would have been amongst the impulsive countryfolk who were Squire Garrett Wesley's tenants in County Meath!

The prim little Fellow of Lincoln must have felt somewhat ruffled by the sudden visits of his brother. 'He would burst in on John in his rooms at Lincoln, recite scraps of poetry, turn over the papers on his desk, peer among them with his near-sighted eyes for what he wanted, and pour out a stream of questions and remarks without waiting for the answers. He was orderly in nothing but his hand-writing, which was exquisite.' So writes his biographer, Miss Dora M. Jones.

It is the picture of a harum-scarum, in whom there is no vice and much attractive virtue. He respected and admired his brother John. At Stanton Harcourt he was welcomed, but was a little subdued, perhaps because he was younger than the rest of the group of friends. He does not seem to have been worried by any thought of the quest on which his brother had set out. Life at Oxford was a great and happy adventure. Every day brought him some new enthusiasm, some new friendship. He accepted such gifts gladly but never selfishly.

Presently John left to take up his curacy at Wroote. What would happen next? Would Charles drift with the stream or was there some sterner stuff in him? The answer came most unexpectedly. Impetuous, careless, unmethodical Charles was face to face with a spiritual crisis. Even in these days, when emotions are analysed and classified with the utmost freedom and confidence, no one has ventured to trace the stages of the process. No one ever can! Suddenly – as though the Divine Love were impulsive too – Charles Wesley was smitten into a new sense of responsibility.

He had missed his brother greatly, and when he realized this strange crisis he wrote to him forthwith: 'God has thought fit (it may be to increase my wariness) to deny me at present your company and assistance. It is through Him strengthening me I trust to maintain my ground till we meet. And I hope that neither before nor after that time I shall relapse into my former state of insensibility. It is through your means I firmly believe, that God will establish what He hath begun in me; and there is no other person I would so willingly have to be the instrument of good to me as you. It is owing in great measure to somebody's prayers (my mother's most likely) that I am come to think as I do, for I cannot myself tell how or when I awoke out of my lethargy, except that it was not long after you went away.'

There is no arrogance here, no trace of priggishness. He soon gathered his friends together to share his experience. It was partial, it is true, but it was definite. The friends began to attend Holy Communion regularly. The change was sudden and it could not pass unnoticed. The little group of men were dubbed 'Sacramentarians', then another word was revived and they were called 'Methodists'. In one of his letters Charles explained that this was because they had 'agreed together to observe with strict formality the method of study and practice laid down in the Statutes of the University'. They began to meet regularly for prayer and Bible-reading.

When John Wesley returned from Wroote he joined the little group. At once he was accepted as its leader. The meetings were held in his room at Lincoln College, on the first floor on the south of the quadrangle. They read their Greek Testament together; they were called Bible Moths! They began by meeting on Sunday evenings but soon they met every night from six to nine o'clock; they were called the Holy Club! They appeared to many to be self-righteous and spiritually arrogant, but they were, in fact, sincere and eager to learn. It is true that they disciplined themselves rigorously, and were punctilious in outward observances, but it is not true to say that they were a handful of selfish young prigs. Amongst them were three respected tutors, and several who proved themselves, in widely differing spheres, men of strong character and nobility of soul.

One of the difficulties of understanding their attitude has been that modern critics have forgotten that the phraseology of the day sounds stilted and pompous two centuries later. They did not claim that they had found what they sought; still less did they remain introspective and selfishly inactive.

They made some attempt to rediscover the practices of primitive Christianity. They were not altogether successful, nor, as some of them learnt later, would the discovery and practice have been the solution to their problems. At the same time it decided their habits. They rose early, spent certain definite hours in prayer, attended Holy Communion every week, repeated a Collect three times each day. They studied the Greek Testament methodically, and lived sparingly, devoting what they saved to charitable work. It is easy to be cynical and suggest that they were smugly anxious to save their own souls but that is not the whole truth.

One of the number, William Morgan, visited the Castle prison to minister to a man condemned to death for the murder of his wife. He brought back a terrible account of the conditions in which the prisoners lived. They were ignorant and hopeless; many of them were imprisoned for debt and were the victims of misfortune. The other members of the Holy Club went to see for themselves. They were dismayed at what they saw! At once they resolved to make regular visitations. It is unfair to suggest that they 'were using the helpless prisoners as raw material on which to practise the zeal that was, they hoped, to save their own souls'. They bought books and medicine and clothes for the prisoners. They scraped together enough to pay the debts of some of them and so to set them free. They taught the illiterate to read – surely a priceless boon. They prayed with them, and celebrated Holy Communion in their midst. What more could they do? They had not yet learnt the secret of a radiant and personal Christian experience themselves, but what they had they gave freely. It is childish to suggest that the medicine was 'compounded by ignorance' and the books 'dictated by superstition'. That is to assume either that the medicine and the books of to-day are perfect and final or to assert that they, also, should be withheld!

Regularly they visited the Bocardo, the debtors' prison, over the north gate of the city. The debtors were a quarrelsome lot, but the Holy Club were not deterred.

In the prison at the Castle, where the criminals were, they seemed to succeed better. They melted the heart of a hardened old sheep-stealer. They encouraged one, Jempro, to read aloud to his fellow-prisoners. We cannot imagine the latter suffering it unless they had enjoyed it. They struggled to teach a horse-stealer to read. He was a slow scholar, but they persevered and taught him his letters. He was eager enough to learn, and one of them went 'to hear his lessons' three times a week.

They were only a handful of men, never more than twenty-seven, and sometimes only five in number, yet they excited the interest of the whole University. The Common Rooms discussed the situation. Many scoffed. Some criticized the austerities severely. A few were impressed. John Clayton, tutor of Brasenose, joined the little band. They extended their activities. Money was gathered from the scanty resources to start a school for the poorest children of Oxford. The children came ill clad and cold. As soon as it was possible the Holy Club bought them clothes.

The old rector watched the progress from afar. 'Bear no more sail than is necessary, but steer steady,' he wrote to John. Varying his metaphor a little he advised Charles, 'You are now fairly launched. Hold up your head and swim like a man'. Brother Samuel wrote from Westminster when he heard of the charges brought against them, 'The charge of enthusiasm can weigh with none, but such as drink away their senses, or never had any. For surely activity in social duties, and a strict attendance on the ordained means of grace, are the strongest guards imaginable against it'.

In spite of unceasing opposition, and many disappointments, the Holy Club persisted. Its members believed they were obeying the divine command and no ridicule or punishment could turn them back. They were rigid and formal in many of their beliefs and practices, but at least they tried to express such religion as they knew in service to the poor and the distressed.

Suddenly the little world of the Wesleys was changed. The old rector was dying and John went as often as he could, afoot or on horseback, to visit him. During these journeys he learnt to read whilst riding, and he kept up the habit for more than forty years.

In 1735 the old man finished his masterpiece on Job, and lay down to die. His son John was thirty-two years old, and to him he committed the volume of six hundred pages to be taken to London to the Queen. This done, he sank to rest, almost content. No more worrying about debts! No more facing angry parishioners! All his little books were finished. The Book of Life was opened. A very gallant little gentleman passed on.

CHAPTER 5

KNIGHT ERRANT

A CRITICAL moment had arrived. The death of the old rector changed many things. With all his failings he had been fixed ground for his family.

There had been the hope that John would take his place at Epworth, but he had refused, supporting his refusal with much argument. His reasoned statement seemed, on the face of it, a little selfish. He preferred the security and opportunity of Oxford. Perhaps the real fact was that he was afraid of Epworth, remembering his failure at Wroote. His experience in the Holy Club had given him some idea of what he could do. Certainly it was not a future of idleness or easy popularity which he craved, but it seems as though he shrank from work which he knew, in his heart, he was unfit to attempt. There was still that sense of something missing. He was struggling to save his own soul. The dull, heavy-hearted folk of his father's parish would not be likely to respond to such a pre-occupied messenger. They needed some one with good news of hope and joy – even of assurance!

Though he relented and gave tacit consent for steps to be taken to secure his appointment, it was too late. The living was vacant but John Wesley was not nominated. The sticks and stools in the old rectory were sold, together with the farm stock. Debts were paid. Susanna moved, with her few personal belongings, to the little school Emilia had started at Gainsborough. John and Charles went back to Oxford, taking the *Dissertations on the Book of Job* with them.

Even Oxford was changed. The members of the Holy Club were scattered. One had become a clergyman at Stanton Harcourt, another was a curate in Essex, a third was chaplain at the Tower, two of the rest were at Manchester, and George Whitefield, the pot-boy of Gloucester, had gone back to evangelize his native town!

The old rector had always been an optimist, but he had never been so certain that he was on the verge of success as when he was hurrying to finish his last book. This was to be his masterpiece. Before he died he made sure his boys would sponsor it. The two brothers, John and Charles, left Oxford and came to London. John had decided to present the book to Queen Caroline herself. It was dedicated to her, and Samuel had staked his hope on her good offices. She was a remarkable personality. At times she would discuss theology with her chaplain or some distinguished divine, at other times she would attempt to share in the gaieties of the Court, and always her first concern was to satisfy the slightest whim of her coarse, ill-mannered husband, lately the Elector of Hanover but now George II of England.

After some weeks, an audience was granted and the solemn young Oxford don, with the large volume under his arm, came to St. James's Palace. The Queen would receive him, and the work of his father would be established. There is something pathetic about the whole scene. He came across the great room, where her Majesty was dallying with her maids of honour, a little timidly but none the less steadfastly. He stood before her, knelt down and offered her the book – his father's crowning work. The Queen smiled, looked at the cover a moment, and then at John Wesley, waiting expectant. 'It is prettily bound,' she lisped, and, with another smile, put the book down on the window-seat. He stood up, bowed low, walked backwards, and in a moment was gone.

It was probably the strangest Sunday of his life. His old father had written a dedication to Queen Caroline, believing that she was 'an encourager of learning', but before John Wesley had reached the palace gate, she was chattering again with her maids of honour. He was not discouraged; he had other things to think about. He was on the edge of a great adventure. However little he and his friends understood the strange quest which disturbed their hearts, it is certain that the lords and ladies of the Court would have understood nothing at all.

During the weeks of waiting, John and Charles had been staying at the house of young James

Hutton, whose father, an Anglican clergyman, now kept a boarding-school in Westminster. Whilst there the three friends discussed their future. There were not many ways that seemed open to John Wesley. He might become a schoolmaster, he might perhaps go back to Oxford or he might settle down in a country living as had his father before him.

Suddenly the whole prospect changed. John Wesley met James Oglethorpe, and within two months was on his way to America to convert the Creek Indians. It seemed an incredibly impulsive decision, but it happened quite naturally.

When the young Oxford Methodist faced the founder of the colony of Georgia he discovered a kindred spirit. The man who had struggled to serve the prisoners in the Bocardo met the man who had fought against great odds to clean up the Fleet, the Marshalsea, and the King's Bench Prisons. How often had Oglethorpe, member of Parliament for Hasle-mere, tried to force the Royal Commissions of which he had been chairman, to face the whole problem! How slow they had been to respond! Meanwhile debtors, with no opportunity of earning money to repay their debts, rotted in pestilential rooms when they were no longer able to pay the extortionate fees of the sponging housekeepers. The best of them lay cheek by jowl with the worst. There was no serious attempt at classification, and no logical process which might lead to deliverance. Jail-fever and small-pox thinned the ranks, and those who survived sank into hopeless gloom. Employment was scarce, and debts inevitable. People went into prison the helpless victims of circumstance. They struggled there with no prospect of getting out. Even the philanthropic folk who tried to relieve them and secure their discharge could offer them no work. It was because of this that Oglethorpe conceived the idea of founding the colony of Georgia. A number of influential men were gathered together and he submitted to them his plan. He proposed that land should be acquired in America, by Charter, and its development vested in a Trust. From the wretched prisoners of the Fleet and Marshalsea some should be chosen and 'transplanted' to Georgia. There, in association with more normal settlers, they might find new hope and new life.

It was not just an excuse for extending what we call the Empire. It was a genuine effort to relieve distress and to bring real opportunity to people who had given up in despair. Religious refugees flying from persecution on the Continent were offered holdings in the new colony. Highlanders, escaping from hardship and starvation, accepted grants of land in return for semi-military duties on the frontier. However the final results may be criticized it is certain that the experiment was sincere and unselfish. There had never been anything quite like it before.

Its progress had been a frequent topic of conversation in the Epworth rectory, and John Wesley saw in Oglethorpe something more than a soldier and empire-builder. To him this trim, straight figure was that of an enthusiast, eager to solve some of the problems with which he, himself, had been grappling.

Probably the Governor of Georgia was equally interested in John Wesley. He had never met him before, but he knew a good deal about his family. Had he not come to the rescue of the harassed little rector on more than one occasion? As soon as he had returned to England the previous year he had been greeted by a letter from him. 'Honoured Sir,' wrote Samuel Wesley, 'It is not only your valuable favours on many accounts to my son Samuel, late of Westminster, and myself when I was a little pressed in the world, nor your extreme charity to the poor prisoners; it is not these only that so much demand my warmest acknowledgements, as your disinterested and unmovable attachment to your country, and your raising a new colony, or rather a little world of your own in the midst of a wild wood and uncultivated desert, where men may live free and happy, if they are not hindered by their own stupidity and folly, in spite of the unkindness of their brother mortals.' Young Samuel had published 'An Ode to James Oglethorpe, Esq., in the Country' and dedicated to him his poem, 'The Prisons Open'd'. A few months before they met, Oglethorpe had used his influence to try to secure the appointment of John Wesley to the living of Epworth. In the List of Subscribers printed in the monumental *Dissertations on the Book of Job*, his name appeared. He had taken 'seven large-paper copies' for which he paid twenty-one guineas. No wonder that he was more than a little intrigued at meeting the son of the importunate old rector, who had won his sympathetic regard.

It was Dr. Burton of Corpus Christi College, Oxford, and one of the Georgia Trustees, who brought John Wesley to see Oglethorpe. He was one of the most useful and energetic members of the Board, and was particularly concerned in the religious development of the new colony. They had not been very fortunate in the ministers who had been appointed and he was very anxious to get the right type of man in the early stages of the experiment. The fact that Wesley was in London gave him an opportunity which Oglethorpe welcomed. At this first interview he asked him, point-blank, whether he would come out to Georgia? It was an unexpected situation for the man who had been hesitating between the seclusion of a school and the security of Oxford. Perhaps he would not have considered it, had it meant merely undertaking the duties of a parish priest amongst the settlers of Savannah. But somebody mentioned the word 'Indian'! That was an entirely different challenge. It made an instant appeal to John Wesley. The Trustees were rightly concerned that the colonists should be God-fearing and disciplined. Oglethorpe had sacrificed popularity because he had set his face sternly against the introduction of negro slave-labour and had forbidden the manufacture and sale of spirits. With such a policy, Wesley was in absolute agreement, but it would not have drawn him from England. It was this dream of converting the Indians which gave him pause. The thought of pioneer work on virgin soil, the dazzling prospect of preaching to unspoilt simple souls – that was an entirely different matter. He went away to think it over.

It was scarcely a year since London had welcomed a little company of Indians. The whole Town had been agog with the excitement. Every coffee-house had discussed the behaviour of Tomochichi and the rest of the Creeks whom Oglethorpe had brought back from Georgia. They had been received somewhat pompously by the Trustees, and Oglethorpe had explained that they had come 'to learn English and the Christian religion and confirm the peace'. The King and Queen had received them at Kensington Palace. It had been an amazing scene. The old chief was arrayed in a fine scarlet robe edged with white rabbit-fur and bordered with gold galloon lace. His wife, Senauki, was resplendent in scarlet, whilst the lesser chiefs wore blue. In spite of protest by the more solemn and unimaginative Trustees, they had insisted on appearing with painted faces! The King had received a gift of eagle's feathers, a pledge of peace. The Queen had heard little Tooanahowi, the fifteen-year-old heir, recite the Lord's Prayer, the Creed and the Ten Commandments! The Archbishop of Canterbury had received them at Lambeth, though as Egmont naïvely remarks in his *Journal*, 'they had apprehensions that he was a conjuror, but the kind reception he gave them altered the imagination'. They had been entertained at Charlton and been duly catechized by their pompous old host, who discovered that they 'held monotheistic beliefs' and had definite views on immortality. He felt 'Providence had prepared them to be Christians'. They gave great joy to the boys at Eton College for Tomochichi begged that they might be given a day's holiday! Treaties were made and in November they set sail again for Georgia.

As Wesley pondered his future he pictured such people in their simple houses of timber and wattle, plastered inside with mud and white-washed with powdered oyster-shells. He remembered that the old chief had told them his father had been burnt by the Spaniards because he would not become a Christian. To bring them the consolation of the Christian faith as he understood it, seemed a better thing than to go back to the fluttering hens and sleepy villagers of Wroote, or even to Oxford, now emptied of his friends. Even as he sat thinking, the Trustees were reading a strange message written on buffalo skin and sent by the Creek tribes to assure the English people of their gratitude and their friendship.

John faced the new situation calmly. There was no question of sudden or sentimental impulse. True to his primitive loyalties he felt he must consult with his brethren! He talked with his brother Charles and Samuel, he talked with William Law, and then rode off to Manchester to see Clayton and Byrom, his Oxford friends. From Manchester he rode to ask advice of Susanna, his wisest counsellor. There was no doubt in her mind at all. The prospect of a son of hers becoming a missionary to the Indians was alluring. 'If I had twenty sons I should rejoice that they were all so employed, though I never saw them more.'

Whilst he was away he received a letter from Dr. Burton, urging him to accept the invitation. Time was pressing, for Oglethorpe was preparing to sail within a month. He made it plain that there was need of men 'inured to contempt of ornaments and conveniences of life, to serious thoughts and bodily austerities'. It was ten days before the answer came, but it made him rejoice. John Wesley was going to Georgia and with him would go his brother Charles, Benjamin Ingham and Charles Delamotte. It was like a little section of the Holy Club that was to be transplanted from the comfortable room at Lincoln

College to the long stretches of 'pine-barren' in the New World.

Before they sailed John Wesley wrote a long letter to Dr. Burton, explaining in his peculiarly candid way the reason for the adventure. 'My chief motive, to which all the rest are subordinate, is the hope of saving my own soul.' Much has been made of the isolated sentence. Whilst it undoubtedly provides a key to the problem of his failure in Georgia, it has generally been exaggerated. The next passage in the letter reads: 'I hope to learn the true sense of the gospel of Christ, by preaching it to the heathen.' He expected to find a simple folk, 'as little lambs, humble, willing to learn'. It was hardly his fault that they proved so different. The whole tone of the letter reveals a mood and motive much less selfish than does the solitary sentence. 'I hope, from the moment I leave the English shore, under the acknow-ledged character of a teacher sent from God, there shall no word be heard from my lips but what properly flows from that character: . . . I then hope to know what it is to love my neighbour as myself, and to feel the powers of that second motive to visit the heathens, even the desire to impart to them what I have received, a saving knowledge of the gospel of Christ.' Even as he writes he hesitates. Does he know enough? Can he himself give what he has not got? 'But', he continues, 'I am assured if I be once (fully) converted myself, He will then employ me, both to strengthen my brethren and to preach His name to the Gentiles, that the very ends of the earth may see the salvation of our God.'

It was not the outpouring of selfishness which more than one writer has suggested. Beneath the desire to save his own soul, lay the passionate desire to preach the gospel. As he packed his few belongings he was thinking of Tomochichi and Tooanahowi and hosts of their brethren, waiting expectantly in their mud-daubed huts for the messenger. He was to be disillusioned, but the disillusionment would reveal his own shortcomings more clearly than those of the Creeks.

The little company climbed aboard the *Simmonds* on October 14, 1735, and John went down into the partitioned cabin in the forecastle. In a few moments he was busily writing in his *Journal*: 'Our end in leaving our native country was not to avoid want, God having given us plenty of temporal blessings, nor to gain riches or honour (which we trust He will ever enable us to look on as no other than dung and dross); but singly this – to save our souls, to live wholly to the glory of God.'

It was a week before the *Simmonds* weighed anchor and sailed from Gravesend. Fitful winds held her up almost as soon as she had passed the Goodwins, and she was delayed again at Cowes awaiting the arrival of H.M.S. *Hawk*, a sloop which was to act as escort.

Aboard the *Simmonds* he discovered a strange world. A third consignment of colonists was on its way to a new life. They had been chosen by the Trustees. Many were there not because they were skilled workmen who would make useful settlers, nor even because they were sturdy and could endure hardship, but rather because they had suffered the penalty of failure and were now being rescued from the miseries of the Fleet or the Marshalsea. It was a mixed company, selected by people who were set on carrying out a philanthropic experiment, rather than ensuring good dividends. The second ship, the *London Merchant*, bore the rest of the emigrants.

Sailors might well have questioned the omens. The two vessels were so long held up in Cowes roads that the passengers ate most of the provisions which were intended for their use on the voyage. More had to be purchased at exorbitant prices and of poor quality. The longer they waited the more stormy their passage was likely to be. Twice they were driven back by contrary winds. The delays exasperated John Wesley, but when, at last, on December 10, they stood down Channel, and he saw the ship sailing seaward, his spirits rose. An eight weeks' voyage lay ahead, but every day would bring him nearer what he was convinced was his divinely ordered task. As the three ships put out, with many others that had been waiting a favourable wind, he thanked God and took courage.

On the second day a Channel gale sprang up and the *Hawk* was separated from her consorts. She never joined them again. The two little ships, each of about 220 tons burden, were left to face the fury of the Atlantic alone.

Meanwhile John Wesley and his three friends had settled down to a fixed routine. It was evident that they intended to exercise spiritual oversight with remorseless care. They began to justify their reputation as Methodists. They must rise at four in the morning and end their work at nine o'clock at night. John must learn German, for there were a number of Moravians amongst the emigrants. Delamotte worked at his Greek. Charles Wesley wrote sermons and Ingham taught the children. Public reading and private instruction followed the midday meal, prayers and the exposition of the Lesson, public catechizing of the children, private prayer, more reading and conversation – even then it was only seven o'clock. Away goes John down the gangway between the cabins in the hold – they called it 'the street' – on his way to the German service. Meanwhile Benjamin Ingham read, to such as liked to listen, on the lower deck. The last hour of the day, the four friends met 'to exhort and instruct one another'. Not much wonder that when they lay down at nine o'clock they slept! No 'roaring of the sea nor motion of the ship could take away the refreshing sleep God gave us'.

Twelve ate at Oglethorpe's table, including some gentlemen whose passage he had paid that he might have them as settlers, the captain and the four young 'Methodists'. Salt meat and vegetables were the staple food of the majority. Wesley became a vegetarian! There was some live-stock and dainties, but Oglethorpe took only ordinary fare. It was hard going yet there was little grumbling and no disorder, save that a small boy was thrashed for eating turnips!

Most of the people were kept busy. When the weather was fair the decks were scoured and washed down with vinegar. Thread, worsted, and knitting-needles were served out to the women, and stockings and caps were knitted for use in the new country. Nearly every day the men were drilled and taught the use of small-arms, for the settlers were expected to do guard duty on the frontiers in case of invasion. From time to time Oglethorpe mustered the company and spoke to them about conditions in Georgia, and their coming opportunities. Several times the two ships were becalmed, and he was rowed over to the *London Merchant* to assure himself of the welfare of its passengers.

Eight weeks at sea in a little ship, crowded with people so different in age, education and temperament, would be a trying experience to any one. There was not much serious trouble, although the 'method' of the four young missionaries was too exacting. Some of the passengers responded readily but others were cynical and two, at least, became malicious. The scheming and hypocrisy of Mrs. Hawkins and Mrs. Welch caused difficulty. John Wesley accepted their posturings and repeated penitence with amazing credulity, though his companions saw them for what they were worth. His iron discipline and intense zeal was not the best method of approach. He had no use for what seemed to him to be trivialities, nor would he believe that these apparent converts could be guilty of intrigue and deceit. The incident had its far-reaching consequences on his whole work in Georgia. It helped at last to convince him of the failure of some of his methods, though he had, as yet, no clue to the secret of success.

Limited diet and rough weather brought illness to many herded in the tiny cabins. Oglethorpe gave up his own room to some of the women. The Wesleys insisted he should have theirs and cheerfully 'lay on the boards'.

It gradually became evident that though Charles Wesley had been chosen as secretary, it was his elder brother who had won Oglethorpe's confidence. One day John went to his cabin and was invited to come in. The Governor was very angry. His servant, Grimaldi, an Italian, had apparently drunk most of his special wine, and he determined that he should be flogged. John Wesley looked at him very calmly as Oglethorpe said, 'I never forgive'. 'Then', said

Wesley, 'I hope, sir, you never sin.' The Governor, who was the soul of chivalry, was rebuked and admitted his fault. He drew out his keys, tossed them to Grimaldi, and said, 'There, take my keys and behave better in the future'.

They had been at sea just over a month when a tremendous storm broke over the ship. The main-sail was split into shreds, great seas poured over the deck, and Wesley, like the majority of the passengers, was terribly afraid. Only one little band of people kept their heads. The Moravians went on quite calmly singing a psalm of praise. Every now and again, in a lull in the wind, their voices were heard in joy and thanksgiving. The mainsail split with a noise like great guns. Spars fell on the deck, rigging lay twisted everywhere, and the waves crashed remorselessly over the bulwarks. Nothing stopped the song of praise from the Germans. When at last the gale died down, Wesley spoke to them. 'Were you not afraid?' he said, and they answered mildly, 'No, our women and children are not afraid to die'. Their courage greatly impressed him. He pointed out first to himself, then to his friends, later to the rest of the passengers, the calm that was born of faith in the hearts of these poor German emigrants. He spoke of it wistfully, as of something he longed for but did not possess.

Storm after storm battered the two ships, but they ploughed their way across the Atlantic, timbers creaking, mainsail and foresail split, and masts strained by the fierce gales. Aboard the *Simmonds* only one thing was certain each day – nothing would interfere with the services, the prayers, the public instruction, and all the details of the inexorable routine established by John Wesley and his friends. It is easy for us to criticize it as superficial, mechanical, and even, in a measure, selfish, but to these men it was the *sine qua non* of religion as they understood it. For them there seemed no other way. To have relaxed, they felt, would have been a base betrayal of their trust.

On Sunday, February 1, they sighted the *Pomeroy,* a ship London-bound from Carolina. By her they sent back letters to their friends. On Wednesday soundings were taken. The depth was only twenty fathoms. By noon the look-out at the mast-head sighted the tree-tops of Georgia. As the ship neared the shore John Wesley read the evening lesson. It contained the sentence: 'A great door and effectual is opened.' He prayed fervently, 'O let no one shut it'. His spirits rose again. He was touched to new enthusiasm as he saw the fair vision of Tybee Roads in the calm beauty of early spring.

Next day they cast anchor near Tybee Island. The sky was clear, the water smooth, and the light of the setting sun cast long shadows from the graceful pines which fringed the shore. It was Paradise to the weather-beaten folk in the *Simmonds*.

Early on Friday morning they landed on Peeper Island. Oglethorpe, in patriarchal fashion, led the whole company to a hillock where they knelt down and gave thanks to God. When he put off in a boat for Savannah it was to John Wesley and John Brownfield that he committed the charge of the people while he was away. The voyage was over, and somewhere in the new land were the Indians whom Wesley hoped to save – Creeks, Choctaws, Cherokees and Chickesaws. He looked down the river towards Savannah and rejoiced.

Meanwhile Oglethorpe, with Charles Wesley, was landing at the little town with its wooden cabins arranged in rectangular blocks, with ample open space between them in case of fire. The freeholders were drawn up stiffly presenting arms, and the little cannon barked a welcome as the Governor stepped ashore. The town stood on top of a slope about forty feet above the level of the river which curved round its base. On this raised plateau, or bluff, running inland for five or six miles, Savannah had been built three years before. Its queer little detached houses, its diminutive fort, its court-house used also as a church, the prison, the store-house, and the public mill rejoiced Oglethorpe's heart. The town was growing, and his dream was beginning to come true.

Sunday dawned on Peeper Island. There was an open space, sheltered by myrtles and cedar-trees, where services had already been held. This day they had with them a visitor, August Gottlieb Spangenberg. He had been a professor at Halle but had been expelled for his theological beliefs. Count Zinzendorf had welcomed him to Herrnhut, and he had been chosen to conduct a little party of Moravian brethren to Georgia.

The morning services were over. Probably Spangenberg had preached. It was an opportunity for John Wesley to share his problems with another. He bared his soul and the Moravian astonished him by hesitating to give his opinion till he had asked two or three questions. 'Have you the witness within yourself? Does the Spirit of God bear witness with your spirit that you are a child of God?' It was an unexpected challenge; perhaps it stirred an echo of the past. Old Samuel had spoken some such words a few hours before he died. 'The inward witness, my son, that is the proof, the strongest proof of Christianity.' The words had perplexed John, fresh from his strenuous efforts at Oxford. They were not less perplexing now. All the routine, and external expressions of obedience had not brought him joy nor even certainty. He was dumb before his questioner. 'Do you know Jesus Christ?' persisted Spangenberg. Very cautiously John answered, 'I know He is the Saviour of the world'. 'True,' said the Moravian patiently enough, but, persistently, he continued, 'but do you know He has saved you?' The reply was unconvincing, 'I hope He has died to save me'. Once

more came a last question, 'Do you know yourself?'
At last John stammered, 'I do'. In his *Journal* he
added, 'But I fear they were vain words'. He listened
to Spangenberg's advice but the memory that remained to torment him for many a day to come was
that insistent question, 'Do you know, yourself?'
The darkness fell on Peeper Island, the woods were
sleeping, the ship lay almost motionless at anchor,
but the zealous young ecclesiastic, the missionary who
hoped to convince the Creeks and Chickesaws, lay
wondering. Did he know? How could he convince
men if he were not, himself, assured?

Nearly a week later he was faced for the first time
with the Indians of whom he had thought so long.
Tomochichi and Senauki came, with their nephew,
two women and three children, aboard the *Simmonds*.
The little clergyman looked at them eagerly. The old
chief, his face painted red, his hair dressed with beads,
behind his ear a scarlet feather, stood with his blanket
wrapped about him, and offered John Wesley his
hand. Senauki, his wife, held out a jar of milk and
one of honey, symbols of their expectation and hope.
They were but children; they must be fed with milk
in simplicity of teaching, and with honey in all
kindliness.

'I am glad you are come,' said Tomochichi,
through his interpreter, a trader's wife. 'When I was
in England, I desired that some would speak the
Great Word to me; and my nation then desired to

hear it. But since then we have all been put into confusion.' He told John, pathetically eager to catch every word, that war was in the air. The French and the Spanish were preparing for battle. Traders, from Carolina, were dealing treacherously with the Creeks. These things did not commend the Christian religion to his tribe. 'Yet I am glad you are come,' he concluded. 'I will go up and speak to the wise men of our nation; and I hope they will hear. But we would not be made Christians as the Spaniards make Christians; we would be taught before we are baptized.'

As he ended, John Wesley, evidently greatly impressed, answered very humbly, 'There is but One, He that sitteth in heaven, who is able to teach man wisdom. Though we are come so far, we know not whether He will please to teach you by us or no. If He teaches you, you will learn wisdom; but we can do nothing'.

There is no trace of arrogance or selfishness in the interview, but rather a certain wistful resignation to the dimly understood purposes of God. Though he was a little less confident, the conversation had not altered his intention of going himself wholeheartedly to the work 'of converting the Indians'.

Within a few days, Oglethorpe, Charles Wesley, and the great majority of the new colonists had sailed for Frederica in four smaller boats. John was left with Ingham, at Savannah. For a month they lodged with the Moravians whose whole mode of life was warmly approved. John was taking his bearings. It was evident that Oglethorpe intended him to stay for a while at Savannah. Like a good soldier, he accepted his orders, and tried to obey them. What if he wandered in the pine-woods, and looked eagerly towards Yamacraw, Irene, and to the vast stretches beyond! He must be patient. God had waited long for the souls of the Indians; he must learn to wait.

His first work lay at Savannah, and though his ideals were high, his methods were very severe and rigid. He was very eager to help everybody, but they must be helped in the way he thought the only way. He was a Protestant, but he was a High Churchman of the old school, and he insisted that they behave as the primitive Christians behaved. Unfortunately he had his own ideas as to what that behaviour was.

On February 22 he baptized a baby, eleven days old, and records the event with complete satisfaction. 'Mary Welch was baptized according to the custom of the first Church, and the rule of the Church of England, by immersion. The child was ill then but recovered from that hour.' The sentence is typical of his attitude in the tragic months at Savannah.

At first he made many friends and preached in the court-house to a full company. He gathered little groups of them into meetings for prayer. He celebrated the Sacrament of Holy Communion regularly.

He taught the children their Catechism, and he worked from morning till night, till one wondered how it was possible for him to stand the strain.

He had gone out expecting to fulfil a mission to Indians. He was now in charge of an amazing parish. There were English, German, and French in Savannah. Saints, far more advanced in their religious experience than himself, were living side by side with failures from the prisons suddenly finding themselves free and often inclined to mistake freedom for licence. There were doubtful traders from Carolina and adventurers to whom the free life of this new country offered temptations they did not intend to resist. John donned his cassock, and went amongst them with the loftiest purpose, but with a rigid conception of duty, and an absolute reliance on his sacerdotal office and the vigorous discharge of priestly functions. Somewhere, hidden beneath his vestments and his elaborate but mechanical 'method' was beating a heart of great gentleness. That was why he was so easily deceived. 'As yet he knew only enough to bring him into a great and holy bondage. He had still to learn the truth that makes men free.' When his emotions were deeply stirred or his affections awakened, he hurried back to test his feelings by a machine! If only there had come into his life at this stage some wise, discerning friend, he might have been saved much misery.

After a time he was called away to settle a quarrel

in Frederica, where Charles had been the victim of
some unscrupulous people. The wife of the surgeon,
Hawkins, and her friend, Mrs. Welch – the two
women who had caused the trouble on the *Simmonds*
– had begun another intrigue.

He went in an open sailing boat called a periagua,
and he describes his voyage: 'I wrapped myself up
from head to foot in a large cloak, to keep off the
sand-flies, and lay down on the quarter-deck. Between one and two I waked under water, and seemed
so fast asleep that I did not find where I was until my
mouth was full of it. Having left my cloak, I know
not how, upon the deck, I swam round to the other
side of the periagua, where a boat was tied, and
climbed up without any hurt more than wetting my
clothes. Thou art the God of whom cometh Salvation; Thou art the Lord by whom we escape death.'

At Frederica he found chaos. Oglethorpe was
anxious about the defences of the town and the
Spanish threats from the frontier. The people were
torn by petty jealousies and dangerous gossip. The
two unscrupulous women had drawn Charles Wesley
into their plot to involve Oglethorpe. He was
chafing at the endless letter-writing from which he
turned only to carry out his religious duties. Men
and women, alike, grumbled at the ceaseless call to
prayers and services 'at the beat of the drum', and the
situation was not improved by John's arrival. He
brought his brother back to Savannah, and took over

the care of Frederica. The gossips found him still easier prey and the result was inevitable. In August Charles sailed for England. He had failed, but he left Oglethorpe with friendly farewells.

The climate had undermined his health. He came to London, ill and despondent, but he busied himself with Georgian affairs, and took great pains to help Oglethorpe in a critical time. It is untrue to say that he cherished nothing but bitter memories of their association.

Presently Ingham also returned to England and stayed there. John was left alone to face his increasingly complicated problems. He saw little of Oglethorpe who was busy in the south. The Indians had proved disappointing. He had discovered that they had been corrupted by avaricious and brutal traders. They grew more bitterly prejudiced against Christianity which they imagined, like so many more intelligent people, to be the religion of all white men. Day after day John put on his cassock and preached to dwindling congregations. He was fearless in his denunciation of the people's sins, but Savannah was being demoralized by the arrival of the most dissolute rogues from Carolina. His contacts with the Moravians and the Salzburghers, settled at Ebenezer a few miles away, were the happiest events of his harassed life.

The final stroke which brought Wesley to the depths came unexpectedly. The store-keeper at

Savannah, William Causton, was also chief magistrate. He was unscrupulous and none too honest, but he had a niece, a charming girl of eighteen. Sophie Hopkey was a regular attendant at the little church. She was fascinated by the cultured and handsome young preacher. He was interested in the eager and intelligent pupil, who came not only to public services but sometimes to the parsonage to receive lessons in the French language. Before he realized what was happening he began to fall in love. Gossips magnified and distorted their friendship. Oglethorpe, with the best intention in the world, tried to force it into marriage. The store-keeper did his utmost to compromise John, and make him wed his niece; it would mean a possible ally if his defalcations were discovered and he were compelled to render account to the Trustees.

Amidst all these complex forces John moved like a little child. With almost incredible innocence he passed through situations which must have scorched and consumed a lesser man, but which would not have arisen with one more worldly-wise.

When he realized the seriousness of the situation he consulted his friends the Germans. Finally he cast lots in what he conceived to be the way of scripture, and of primitive Christianity. The fatal slip emerged: 'Think of it no more,' he read. That, for him, was the end. There could be no argument. A year afterward he looked back, and the memory of Sophie brought poignant longing. He was back in England, then, and she was married to another.

Within a few days of realizing his irrevocable decision she gave herself to one, Williamson, and disaster followed. Wesley, accusing her of deceit and neglect of religious duties, refused her permission to attend Holy Communion. Her uncle seized the opportunity to get rid of this man who would now be a menace rather than an ally. It was not difficult to rally forces against him. His rigid discipline and high morality had made him unpopular amongst the riff-raff of Savannah, whose conduct he constantly criticized. The store-keeper influenced Williamson to prosecute Wesley for defamation of his wife's character. He was tried by a grand jury, made up of men picked by Causton. He was found guilty of many breaches of canon law, and finally of defamation. They did not dare to arrest him, and kept postponing his final trial. His work had become impossible. There was nothing to do but set out for England.

He was nothing if he was not methodical. One can see him, nailing up a notice in the public square at Savannah on which were these words: 'Whereas John Wesley decides shortly to set out for England, this is to desire those who have borrowed any books of him to return them as soon as they conveniently can to John Wesley.'

The magistrates demanded a bond, compelling

him, under a penalty of fifty pounds, to appear before
the Court when required. Indignantly he refused to
give it. They replied by publishing an order requiring all officers to prevent his departure. He made his
decision quickly. He would leave at once, but first
he must take evening prayers! At eight o'clock he
was ready to leave Georgia 'after having preached the
gospel . . . not as I ought but as I was able, one year
and nearly nine months'.

He set out in the darkness to make his way to
Charlestown. It was a weary tramp to Port Royal
through miles of barren land. He left on Friday night
and reached Beaufort on Wednesday, after suffering
considerably from hunger and thirst. At last, on the
following Tuesday he got to Charlestown, and
eventually sailed for England in a boat called the
Samuel, on Christmas Eve 1737.

The voyage home was momentous. He never forgot that he was a minister of God, and took the
services regularly on the ship, though his heart was
'sorrowful and very heavy'. When he tried to talk
with the sailors, he found himself tongue-tied. He
persevered, and presently attempted to instruct two
negroes and a poor Frenchman in the Scriptures.

In his solitude and despair he began to realize
things he had missed. He was remorseless, as ever, in
his self-examination. Storms struck the ship, but they
were gentle breezes, compared with the tempest that
raged in his heart.

He wrote down, fearlessly, the secrets of his own soul. He had gone to America to convert the Indians, but he confessed that he was not converted himself. He longed to be a Christian, but he began to wonder if he had not laid too much stress on outward works. He had striven to enforce the practices of primitive Christianity with only a hazy knowledge of what they were.

His weary hand writes the words that burn his brain. 'I have thrown up my friends, reputation, ease, country. I have put my life in my hands, wandering into strange lands; I have given my body to be devoured by the deep, parched up with heat, consumed by toil and weariness or whatever God shall please to bring upon me. . . . Does all I ever did, or can, know, say, give, do or suffer, justify me in His sight? . . . The faith I want is a sure trust and confidence in God that through the merits of Christ my sins are forgiven . . . I want that faith which none can ever have without knowing it.'

Evening fell. It was very calm. Another ship outward bound, sailed slowly past them. It bore George Whitefield to America. The *Samuel* lay becalmed, till suddenly a north wind blew, and presently they dropped anchor off Deal.

The knight errant had reached a stage further in his quest. There are those who see him farther from his goal than ever, but he had begun to realize his mistakes; he was on the way to discover truth. He was not down and out. He stepped ashore from the ship's boat, made his way to the inn and took morning prayers in the common-room before breakfast. Then he set out for London, unafraid, expectant.

CHAPTER 6

THE WONDERFUL BIRTHDAY

IMMEDIATELY after breakfast he rode from the inn at Dover. He must get to London to report to the Georgia Trustees. At nightfall he had reached Faversham. If we accepted the view of some biographers, we should expect him to shrink into the shadows of the room he had hired and to busy himself with morbid introspection or maudlin recollection. Actually you would have found him preaching to the people at the inn! His heart was aching, his mind was perplexed with depressing problems, but there was an inner Voice that would not be denied. He read prayers and expounded 'the Second Lesson to a few of those who were indeed more savage in their behaviour than the wildest Indians I have yet met with'. He did not know all he had longed to know, but he was sure enough of something the loiterers about the tavern needed, and what he had he gave.

Next day he journeyed to Blendon Hall, near Bexley, where he 'expected a cold reception'. He was coming back, utterly conscious of failure and defeat, but he was no coward. He might so easily have avoided such contacts; instead he sought them. There is no trace of ignominious surrender in his attitude. He is a knight on a desperate quest. The Delamottes welcomed him gladly; he was very thankful but he did not stay to nurse his wounds. In the evening he reached London. His brother Charles hurried to James Hutton's to meet him. The time of his outward loneliness had passed.

There was a home for him with the Rev. John Hutton in Westminster, or in the rooms at the 'Bible and Sun', the bookshop kept by his friend, James. Friends were eager to meet him again. They had heard something about the new colony from Charles, but they waited anxiously for John's story. He did not shrink from the ordeal. His spirit was battered and bruised, but he told them the facts plainly. They heard his account with some astonishment but he was restless. He must report his presence in London to the people who had sent him abroad. Several times he went to the offices of the Georgia Trust but it was some days before he had an opportunity of presenting his case and returning his official appointment. They preserved in their 'Journals' a masterly silence beyond the curt recording of facts. Oglethorpe, who was in London, was anxious lest John should, in self-justification, denounce the whole experiment in Georgia. He did nothing of the kind. Life in America was a blurred memory, with a few incidents and people sharply defined. He would not soon forget Sophie Hopkey, nor Oglethorpe, but perhaps the deepest impression had been left by the Moravians who had so constantly challenged his whole conception of religion. They had made him quite certain that he lacked the sense of assurance which was so real to them. His spiritual resources had not been enough to meet the demands of his own life. There was the constant call to preach, and he longed for a more vital gospel. The next four months were spent on this intensified quest, and there are at least five dates which mark stages in his progress.

On Tuesday, February 7, he went to the house of Weinantz, a Dutch merchant, where he met several young Germans who had just landed. It was, as he said, 'a day much to be remembered', for he was introduced to Peter Böhler, a Moravian on his way to begin mission-work in America. The two men became intimate companions. They had much in common, and John Wesley lost no opportunity of talking with him, though the conversation was generally in Latin. He secured lodgings for the little company, near John Hutton's in Westminster. Peter and he went to Oxford together, talking continually of the meaning of faith. Hour after hour Wesley tried to reach Böhler's conclusions by argument. It was impossible. At length the Moravian saw the difficulty. 'My brother,' he said, 'that philosophy of yours must be purged away.' All his life he had been trying, as his father said, 'to carry everything by dint of argument'. The persistent unconscious egotism of the man who would define the infinite within the frontiers of a few Latin words was crowding out faith and bolting the door against personal experience.

Back again he rode to London, and a week later took coach to Salisbury, where he saw his mother, intending to go on to brother Samuel at Tiverton. Suddenly an S.O.S. altered all his plans – perhaps changed his whole career. Word came that Charles lay critically ill, with pleurisy, at Oxford. He had never been well since he left Georgia, and now he was laid low. John hurried back to Oxford – and, providentially, to Peter Böhler. The journey took two days, and on the way he tried to clear his mind on many things. He re-wrote his own account of the Sophie Hopkey episode, and this probably led him to consider his own future conduct. He resolved to be open and unreserved in conversation, to labour after continual seriousness, to speak no word which did not tend to the glory of God, and to guide his pleasures by the same principle. Poor John! still struggling by little codes of rules to reach a shining goal! So he came to Oxford, to find his brother recovering and Peter Böhler preaching joyously of saving faith. Once again he clutched the little page of rules in his pocket, and admitted they were not enough.

On Sunday, March 5, he came to a second crisis. In desperation he had almost decided not to preach again. He went to Böhler to confirm his own feeling that he could not preach to others because he had not faith himself. The young Moravian was quite definite. 'Preach faith till you have it; and then, because you have it, you will preach faith.' It was a somewhat strange command, but S. T. Coleridge defends it by suggesting that 'much may be said where the moral interest of mankind demands it and reason does not countermand; or where the Scripture seems expressly to affirm it'. That explains Wesley's acquiescence. He could see no logical denial of assurance or saving faith; indeed, his eager pursuit of its reality in his own experience, showed his belief in its value. He began to preach it next day. It was no more casuistry than for a partially blind man to advocate the value of seeing clearly, though he himself lived in a misty world.

For some weeks after this he rode from place to place preaching. His texts at this time are illuminating. He was following his friend's advice and proclaiming the reality of faith and its consequences. So he came back to Oxford and found himself in Mr. Fox's Society or fellowship-meeting, with his heart so full that as he says, 'I could not confine myself to the forms of prayer which we were accustomed to use there. Neither do I purpose to be confined to them any more; but to pray indifferently, with a form or without, as I may find suitable to particular occasions'.

This was a great decision for the precise and

rule-bound 'Methodist'. It brought him to a new stage in his quest.

On Easter Sunday, April 2, he preached in Lincoln College chapel. The text was significant and his comment more so. The date marks another milestone. Three times that day, in the beautiful chapel, in the Castle prison, and at Carfax, the home of the Broughtons, he preached on the same verse: 'The hour cometh, and now is, when the dead shall hear the voice of the Son of God, and they that hear shall live.' At night he wrote in his *Journal*: 'I see the promise; but it is afar off.'

It is evident that he felt a crisis was at hand, for he continued in his next sentence, 'Believing it would be better for me to wait for the accomplishment of it in silence and retirement, on Monday the 3rd I complied with Mr. Kinchin's desire and went to him at Dummer, in Hampshire'. A fortnight later he returned to London, still in the same frame of mind.

On Sunday, April 23, he reached another definite stage in the quest. On Saturday he had spent some hours with Peter Böhler, in what the latter described as 'a right searching conversation'. The subject was the same as ever, and John went so far as to agree with his friend that faith was 'a sure trust and confidence which a man has in God, that through the merits of Christ his sins are forgiven and he reconciled to the favour of God'. He agreed too that happiness was a proper result of such a faith. There was one point, however, which still troubled him. Böhler insisted that the coming of such an experience might be instantaneous. He went back to his New Testament, and was astonished to find that most of the instances of conversion, especially in the Acts of the Apostles, were apparently sudden. One last citadel remained, and on Saturday night he retreated within it: Such things happened long ago but times had changed. One could scarcely expect them to occur now!

Next morning even that stronghold was besieged and taken. Böhler brought four Englishmen to bear their witness to the reality of saving faith in their own lives. He watched the effect of their stories on John who was 'thunder-struck'. Still he obstinately said four were only four! Böhler replied he would bring him eight more. John capitulated. He wrote tersely but completely, 'Here ended my disputing. I could now only cry out, "Lord, help Thou my unbelief"!' Together the little group stood up and sang a German hymn:

> My soul before Thee prostrate lies;
> To Thee, her source, my spirit flies;
> My wants I mourn, my chains I see;
> O let Thy presence set me free!

It was a prayer which came from the depths. There was no posturing in that little room. The Moravian saw his friend's eyes were blinded with tears. The tears were there because he had caught a glimpse of the Promised Land, yet could not see the path his feet must tread to reach it.

The next few weeks were not spent in idleness. He spoke continually of the subject that was in his heart. Three days before sailing Peter Böhler met the two Wesleys, Piers, the vicar of Bexley, and certain others at the 'Bible and Sun'. A society was formed for fellowship, rather on the lines of a modern Group. It began with simple rules, which were unfortunately multiplied later when it moved to Fetter Lane. On Wednesday Peter Böhler convinced Charles of the nature of that living faith by which 'through grace we are saved'. On Thursday, May 4, the young Moravian had gone. In his few months' stay in London he had helped to change the course of English history. Little did he think as he wrote a few lines to John, urging him to believe in *his* Jesus Christ, that he had led his friend to the brink of a new experience from which should be born a great revival. Nor did John realize how far he had, himself, come. It was only three months since he first met Böhler. For nine weeks he had argued, not so much with the Moravian as with himself. The arguments were ended but the experience seemed as far off as ever. Some days he was 'sorrowful and heavy'. He could neither pray nor read; he could not think or sing. He was at the far end. At other times he went out bravely to preach about the faith he did not yet know in its fullness.

There was a certain urgency about his preaching, now, which attracted the people and frightened the clergy. His message was personal and vital. The people did not hear a polished essay. They were fascinated by this man who had not brought a sermon in his pocket, but spoke to them directly. Just at the moment when his words seemed to be more effective than ever before, the church doors were closed to him. Place after place was forbidden. He had not been surprised, in those first breathless days after his return from Georgia, that his passionate words had given offence. In February he had been forbidden to preach again in St. John the Evangelist's, Westminster, and in St. Andrew's, Holborn. Now it became almost customary. He seemed to be preaching a round of farewell sermons. The list grew longer. He must not preach any more in St. Lawrence's, St. Katherine Cree's, Great St. Helen's, St. Ann's, Aldersgate, St. John's, Wapping or St. Benet's. It was not encouraging. Some of his old friends were dismayed as much by his manner as by his doctrine. He went on steadfastly, without any great joy but in spite of periods of real depression. His heart might break, but as long as he could, he would preach the gospel as he understood it. That was the difficulty. It was still, largely an intellectual process though it was passionate enough in its sincerity.

Though Charles Wesley had not accepted Böhler's teaching till the night before he sailed, it soon became more than mere acquiescence. For some time he had been lodging with Bray, a poor brazier living in Little Britain, near Aldersgate. He was only partly recovered from his pleurisy and on May 19, lay ill. One of the Moravians, William Holland, a painter, visited him and described the incident: 'Being providentially directed to Martin Luther's *Commentary on the Epistle to the Galatians*, I carried it round to Mr. Charles Wesley, who was then sick at Mr. Bray's.' It was a revelation. Charles found Martin 'nobly full of faith'. His visitor left and he lay thinking. Again and again he returned to the comments on the last verses of the second chapter. Presently he was repeating, not Luther but Paul, 'Who loved me and gave himself for me'. If only he could realize that 'me' meant Charles Wesley! He 'laboured, waited and prayed to feel' it. On Whit-Sunday, May 21, his prayer was answered.

Brother John had been to St. Mary-le-Strand to hear Dr. Heylyn preach. He had assisted him at Holy Communion. After the service he was told about what had happened. 'I received the surprising news that my brother had found rest to his soul. His bodily strength returned also from that hour. Who is so great a God as our God?'

Lonelier now than ever, John struggled on. Twice that day he preached, and on each occasion was told that he must preach no more in that church. His own heart was heavy. He tried to escape its repressions by writing a letter to a friend. It was a passionate cry that he might be saved from trusting in anything but his Saviour.

On Tuesday morning, May 23, Charles writes, 'I waked under the protection of Christ and gave myself up, soul and body, to Him'. The whole world was new. He must get up. He must write. He must sing – yes, that was it, he must sing. There was too much for one song – too much for six thousand, though God was to spare him to write them. Pen! Paper! Ink!

> Where shall my wondering soul begin?
> How shall I all to heaven aspire?
> A slave redeemed from death and sin,
> A brand plucked from eternal fire,
> How shall I equal triumphs raise,
> Or sing my great Deliverer's praise?

The pen flew on over the waiting paper. It must surely scorch the page. Eight verses are written, sung for very joy. It is the song of a soul, believing itself new-born – but it swells into a universal call to all men to share with him this great, redeeming love.

> Outcasts of men, to you I call,
> Harlots, and publicans, and thieves!

Somewhere, walking the streets of London, John trudges on patiently, expectantly, wondering. The hours pass, he goes home to bed. For him there is no song – only a hunger that cannot be satisfied. Day broke over London on Wednesday, May 24, 1738, and the growing light stole in through the windows, waking the sleepers to begin once more the round of work. There was nothing to let them know their little lives would be altered by the happenings. Nobody dreamt that before nightfall something would come to pass which would change the course of history. Only one man could have told them what had happened to him.

'I think it was about five this morning, that I opened my Testament on those words: "There are given unto us exceeding great and precious promises, even that ye should be partakers of the divine nature" (2 Pet. i. 4). Just as I went out, I opened it again on those words, "Thou art not far from the kingdom of God". In the afternoon I was asked to go to St. Paul's. The anthem was, "Out of the deep have I called unto Thee, O Lord: Lord hear my voice. O let Thine ears consider well the voice of my complaint. If Thou, Lord, wilt be extreme to mark what is done amiss, O Lord, who may abide it? For there is mercy with Thee; therefore shalt Thou be feared. O Israel, trust in the Lord: for with the Lord there is mercy, and with Him is plenteous redemption. And He shall redeem Israel from all his sins".

'In the evening I went very unwillingly to a society in Aldersgate Street, where one was reading Luther's preface to the *Epistle to the Romans*. About a quarter before nine, while he was describing the change which God works in the heart through faith in Christ, I felt my heart strangely warmed. I felt I did trust in Christ, Christ alone for salvation; and an assurance was given me that He had taken away *my* sins, even *mine*, and saved *me* from the law of sin and death.'

It was an amazing day. The very first words had leaped at him from the printed page. He had been stirred into new wakefulness. He opened the book again – 'not far from the Kingdom of God'. He went out to walk the streets. He was lonely, distraught. A friend persuaded him to go to the great Cathedral. The anthem was as the cry of his own soul. Old Dr. Crofts had understood, and the very music cried out for him. He groped his way out of the dimly-lit church. His soul was in travail.

Restless, dissatisfied with himself, and uneasy because of the strange stirrings on his heart and mind, he wandered on. It was already evening. Unwillingly he dragged his feet towards the narrow byway on the East side of Aldersgate. In a little room in Nettleton Court the 'society' was assembling. Why should he go? Why must he go? He is in their midst – the picture of dejection. Presently, honest William Holland stands up to read. He listens, dully at first, then more intently. Something happens. He is radiantly happy. His heart is warm, aflame! 'I began to pray with all my might for those who had in a

more especial manner despitefully used and perse-
cuted me.' Joy! doubt! buffetings! victory! He cannot contain it. All the world must know – but first
Charles. Round the corner he runs. His friends can
scarcely keep up with him. Up the stairs in the
brazier's house in Little Britain, they clamber.
Charles is waiting. 'I believe', cries John. Not
another word! He would not have been heard, had
he uttered it. They are all singing the new hymn:

> Where shall my wondering soul begin,
> How shall I all to heaven aspire?

It is a birthday – one of the great birthdays in the
history of the world.

What shall we say of it all? Was he not a good man
before? Can this be conversion? Was it not rather
his evangelical conversion? Was it an awakening, an
illumination, a revelation, 'something tidal', or shall
we sneer and count it hysteria, the emotional product
of fear? Best perhaps let words alone. Let it speak
for itself. Here is a man transformed. In his troubled
heart, deep peace at last. In his whole being strange
new energy. Fifty years of amazing activity beginning. Fire running through stubble. The grace of
God in England.

Was it a birthday? Was he not a good man before?
He was so conscientious and painstaking that he
might have become a model cleric if he had missed
out this day. He had been a faithful priest; he

became a flaming prophet. He had been a dutiful servant; he became a joyful son.

There would be days of depression and seeming defeat, but never again would he forget that *he* was forgiven – that God was with *him*.

"Thursday, 25. – The moment I awaked, "Jesus, Master" was in my heart and in my mouth.'

'If any man be in Christ he is a new creature.'

CHAPTER 7

STRANGE CATHEDRALS

THREE weeks after his great experience John Wesley set out for Germany. Had he been the crazy victim of a mere emotional upheaval we should look for him in the midst of a London mob, which would have found considerable delight in baiting a madman. Had he been a fanatic, exulting in the belief that he had suddenly escaped the fires of hell, we should expect to find him immediately exhorting the crowds and driving them in a frenzy of fear to flee from the wrath to come.

The picture is entirely different. Deliberately, but eagerly, he makes his preparations for a quiet pilgrimage. No one had more constantly challenged the quality of his faith than the Moravians he had met in America and England. The courage of the little group of emigrants aboard the *Simmonds*, the persistent questioning of Spangenberg and the tireless concern of Peter Böhler had spurred him on his quest. To these people he owed much and from them he was still prepared to learn. His heart had been strangely warmed but he had not lost his sense of proportion. Fellowship with the Moravian Societies would confirm or correct and interpret his new-found faith.

On his journey to Marienborn, where he met Count Zinzendorf, and on his long tramp to Herrnhut he was as keenly observant and as critically analytical as ever. The journey itself was not easy going. He tramped along, with Benjamin Ingham, eyes wide open, mind alert. Passes must be continually produced and *bona fides* established. At Halle, the King of Prussia's 'tall men' challenged the travellers, at the gates. For two hours they were sent from guard to guard, none being prepared to admit them. But when they did get in they saw the Orphan House and saw it so completely that it became the pattern for orphanages all over nineteenth-century England!

At Neustadt they were refused lodgings, and trudged wearily to the next town where they found 'a sort of inn. But they told us plainly we should have no lodgings with them, for they did not like our looks. About eight we were received at a little house in another village, where God gave us sweet rest'.

Next day they came to Herrnhut, where Wesley found Mr. Hermsdorf, an old friend whom he had met in Georgia. The little community received him graciously but without any ceremony or excitement. At once he began to attend their services, to talk with all whom he met concerning their religious experience, to visit the school, and to study carefully the constitution of the whole society. He was still precise and accurate, classifying and analysing his results, little dreaming how vast were the consequences of this personal pilgrimage.

At Marienborn his verdict had been, 'I continually met with what I sought for, viz., living proofs of the power of faith'. At Herrnhut he found a community which thrilled him. All its members seemed to share a common experience of great joy. He wrote enthusiastically to Samuel: 'God has given me at length the desire of my heart. I am with a Church whose conversation is in heaven, in whom is the mind of Christ, and who walk as He walked.' Here was a vital experiment being tried out. A little society existed within the Church, not separated from it. Such communities might be extended in the Church of England. Perhaps God would use him in some such way. He stayed long enough to collect his material and then regretfully bade farewell to Christian David, the carpenter pastor and his friend. 'I would gladly have spent my life here; but my Master calling me to labour in other parts of His vineyard, I was constrained to take my leave of this happy place.'

He turned homewards with a stronger and more informed faith. There were certain features of the Moravian experiment which he criticized but there were more which he accepted. He began to see how saving faith might be applied to English life, and how the Moravian methods might be adapted to the English temperament.

The fellowship meetings at Herrnhut were the models for early Methodist Bands and Classes. A conference he attended at Marienborn became the pattern on which several of the first Methodist Conferences were planned. Lovefeasts and Watch-nights were copied from meetings held at Herrnhut, which were themselves based on the agapæ and vigiliæ of the early Christian Church.

He was back again in London on September 16, having been away three months. Next day, being Sunday, he preached three times and on Monday visited the condemned prisoners in Newgate.

It seems almost an anti-climax after the peak experience in May. The educative and ordered tour on the Continent was followed by months of preaching in such churches as would tolerate his intense evangelistic zeal. Almost obscurely, and with no idea of the vastness of the work he was soon to accomplish, he went on preaching wherever he could. He soon learnt that he must not divide his message into two sermons for morning and evening, because frequently the incumbent was so alarmed at the first discourse that he refused him a second opportunity.

Soon the whole situation was changed. Church doors were closed and he found himself preaching in a cathedral built by God! It was George Whitefield who brought him face to face with the new situation.

Whitefield, son of the landlady of the Bell Inn at Gloucester, had been a servitor at Oxford when the

Wesleys were there. Poor and ill-equipped he had struggled to pick up what learning he could. He became a member of the Holy Club, was ordained and began to preach. Almost at once his dramatic power attracted attention. The day John Wesley landed in England, he sailed for Georgia. For a few months he preached in the American colonies, raising money for the orphanage he had determined to build.

He soon returned to England and people flocked to hear him. Unfortunately his preaching was much more emotional than John Wesley's and in February 1739, his enemies began to complain of the disorder caused by his services. The church doors shut with a decided bang. It was a bitter winter but he went with great confidence to preach to the colliers at Kingswood. Crowds listened to him eagerly. On Saturday afternoon, February 18, 1739, he spoke to 'five or six thousand persons at Hanham Mount, and in the evening held another meeting on the Common, half a mile away. People came in coaches, on horse-back, and afoot. The crowd covered three acres and numbered twenty thousand. Their presence was a challenge'. Whitefield realized that this work must go on. He was preparing to return to America. There was no one in the Bristol area who could take his place as a field-preacher. What could be done? At once his thoughts turned to John Wesley, who was preaching in whatever churches he could, and work-ing hard amongst the religious societies in London, especially at Fetter Lane. He sat down and wrote a letter appealing to him to come to Bristol at once.

John Wesley was staying at Bray's in Little Britain, though he spent many hours each day at Mr. Agutter's, where in the quiet of the Charterhouse precincts he could study and write.

The letter caused upheaval. Scriptural passages were read. Brother Charles and the Fetter Lane Society were consulted and the general opinion was that John's health was bad and he should not go. None of the arguments, still less his own reluctance, were conclusive. Once more they resorted to the primitive method of casting lots. On March 29 he mounted his horse and rode out towards Bristol. Two days later he arrived at the city, having ridden hard from Basingstoke.

It was Saturday and people thronged the streets, marketing. Carefully he guided his tired horse through the rows of stalls and barrows in the narrow, twisted roads. At last he turned its head up Wine Street. Horse was weary and rider was unwilling. Those last few yards were the worst! Past the whipping-post and the pillory he went, slowly enough, and at last dismounted outside a little grocer's shop.

Why was he there? He might have been quietly reading in his rooms at Lincoln College. Customers came in and out making their Saturday night purchases. He did not hear their chatter. In the semi-darkness of the room beyond he was thinking hard.

All his life – till very lately – he had been an advocate of decency and order. Field-preaching would have seemed a strangely vulgar business. Had he not satisfied himself, over and over again, that souls must be saved in a church! But the churches were shut against him and the souls, for whom he had this burning message, were unsaved.

The door opens. Whitefield comes in, radiant with the joy of the messenger who has delivered his message. His sister, Mrs. Greville, joins them. They sing and pray together. At eight o'clock they go out again. The horse is resting in its stall, but the rider has not yet ended his day. He hears Whitefield preach at Weaver's Hall, then they return to the little room behind the shop. The tent where Napoleon planned a great campaign, the cabin where Nelson talked with his captains on the eve of Trafalgar are unimportant places in comparison with this council chamber! Till midnight these two talk and pray and talk again. The arguments which have hindered John's decision are overcome by the facts of the situation. The Chancellor of the diocese may protest, the Bishop pause perplexed, but the people come through stormy winter weather! The little Fellow of Lincoln may remember his old prejudices and natural reluctance, his body may object as strongly as his mind, but the miners and the quality have waited side by side, to hear the word. It is impossible to refuse to be the messenger. His arguments are ended, but once again he has not the joy of positive acceptance.

Down on their knees they go – young George Whitefield and John Wesley, thirteen years his senior – and they commend the whole matter to God. They left all things with their Master, and slept.

The morning came – an April Sunday, big with possibilities! He will see and hear for himself. To the bowling-green, in the Pithay, the crowd has come and Whitefield preaches, whilst Wesley listens, keenly alert and anxious to hear that other Voice, above his friend's, commanding him. The service ends, and they set out for Hanham and Kingswood.

Once the countryside has been beautiful, a royal park blessed by a thousand trees. Now it is a wilderness of coal-pits, scores and scores of them on all hands. Rows of colliers' dwellings, little better than black sheds, offer comfortless shelter to the miners. There are no schools for the children, no kind of religious service or teaching for these tired, poverty-stricken workers.

Over the waste ground, with its old tree-stumps and struggling scrub, past the slag-heaps and the pitiful hovels, George Whitefield and John Wesley trudge to the Mount. A tremendous crowd opens up a pathway for them. In a few moments they are all singing a hymn of praise. Presently they are listening spellbound to the young messenger, not so many years removed from the washing of tankards in the scullery of the Bell. The multitude is stirred to new hope as they hear the certainties the preacher, himself, has proved. The service ends, and the friends tramp on again, through the remnants of the wood, with its stunted trees, to Rose Green.

A still bigger crowd has gathered. Coaches are drawn up on its fringe, horses are tethered, but the people, rich and poor alike, press eagerly round the man who has come to speak to them. The wind is fitful, and does not help to carry his voice to their eager ears. He prays for 'strength to cry aloud' and so preaches his farewell sermon.

Farewell! As the people cluster round Whitefield to wish him God-speed, John Wesley realizes the challenge more strongly than before. How can he leave this hungry multitude unfed? It is a day of decision for him – and yet he cannot decide.

That night Whitefield goes to preach to the Religious Society at Baldwin Street. He must take his leave of them before he sails. Down the little back lane he turns, and tries to enter the yard. It is packed with people. Someone brings a ladder. He climbs up, struggles to the roof of the next house and at last clambers into the room. He is sure enough of the rightness of it all. How can he doubt? The people listen to his words in tense silence. At the end of the service, he reminds them of his departure, and announces, simply, that John Wesley will preach next day 'in the brick-yard at the further end of St. Philip's

Plain'. It is an historic proclamation! Whether it was authorized or not, no man can tell.

Meanwhile John had gone alone, to speak to a little company gathered in a room in Nicholas Street. This was more like his proper environment! There was quietness and peace here. Why should a man go out into the fields to face the mob? Strange, that God should have given him his text. Even as he began to expound it, he knows he cannot escape its challenge. It is the Sermon on the Mount – 'a pretty remarkable precedent of field-preaching', he admits to himself as he thinks about it.

The day is nearly over. In the room behind the shop in Wine Street, the friends are met again. They review the events of the past few hours. To-morrow Whitefield will be gone; to-morrow the people will wait in vain for a messenger and the Message unless – there is no avoiding the alternative – unless John Wesley accepts the invitation. He cannot reject it. He hates the prospect. For many a year he hated it. 'To this day', he writes in the *Journal*, 'field-preaching is a cross to me. But I know my commission, and see no other way of preaching the Gospel to every creature.' That night he made the great decision. They did not go to bed at once. How could they? At eleven o'clock they were assembled at Mr. Deschamps's house, for communion, prayer and singing. It was one o'clock when they returned to Wine Street.

Next morning Whitefield rode off to Gloucester,

where he had determined to preach before he sailed for America. John Wesley was left alone to face his great ordeal. First he wrote a long letter to the Fetter Lane Society, then he set out for the brick-yard at the farther end of St. Philip's Plain. Three thousand people were waiting on the clay banks. On a little eminence he stood up, 'submitting to be more vile' as he felt, and there preached his first sermon in the open air in England. His text was: 'The Spirit of the Lord is upon me, because He hath anointed me to preach the gospel to the poor; He hath sent me to heal the broken-hearted, to preach deliverance to the captives, and recovery of sight to the blind, to set at liberty them that are bruised, to preach the acceptable year of the Lord.'

It was a great day for John Wesley, for England and for the whole Christian Church. He records it quite simply, little realizing the amazing consequences of his decision. His diary reflects his feelings. He had risen that day at 7 a.m. 'singing, within'. On Tuesday, with the ordeal over and the step irrevocably taken, he rises at 5.45 and sings as he dresses! The warmed heart will not be denied. He did not like field-preaching, any more than Livingstone liked the fever-swamps of Central Africa, but he did like the certainty of knowing he was doing the will of God. He was not the man to draw back when once he had the assurance that a way, however dangerous or distasteful, was God's way.

He was committed to the work of a field-preacher now and he would need no compulsion. Within a few days he had spoken to many thousands in the open air – at Baptist Mills, at Hanham Mount in Kingswood, and at Rose Green. These were all places where Whitefield had preached. Within a week he had advanced a little. He rode to Bath and preached in a meadow on the side of the hill close to the town; a little later in the day he stood on the steps of a house in Gracious Street and proclaimed forgiveness of sin to the casual passers-by.

Surely April 2, 1739, was one of the most important dates in the story of the Knight of the Burning Heart. That day he made up his mind that the whole world was to be his parish and that he would preach in those cathedrals whose floors were the cobble-stones of market-places or the slag-heaps about a pit-head, the deck of a ship or the rough ground in the corner of a field – cathedrals whose boundaries were hedges or walls or the sea-shore, and whose roof was the blue dome of heaven, built and consecrated by God.

One of the most interesting ceremonies in the Methodist Church, is the Induction of the President. Each year, when the new President takes up his duties, the retiring President hands to him not a gold mace or a regal chain or some brilliant regalia signifying that he is the head of an Order, but he gives him a little, worn, pocket Bible; it is the one John Wesley used on his field-preaching.

Important, however, as the decision to preach in the open air had been, it did not absolve him from its further obligations. He could never become just a wayfaring preacher, content to talk an hour to a crowd and ride away. He was profoundly concerned for the future of the people who were moved to a new beginning. What was to happen to them when he left? Conversion was, after all, an introductory experience.

He had already helped James Hutton to re-organize some of the Religious Societies in London, and he began a similar work in Bristol. Little groups of people were gathered into bands. The Societies meeting in Baldwin Street and Nicholas Street were encouraged and helped in the development and growth of a common experience. They grew in grace and in numbers. The rooms would not hold them. He bought a little piece of land between Broadmead and the Horsefair, and in May 1739, the foundation-stone of 'the new room' was laid. It was a simple building, and by June 3, he was able to hold a service of dedication in it, before he left Bristol for London. In the morning he had preached to six thousand people at Hanham Mount, in the afternoon to eight thousand at Rose Green. 'In the evening', he writes, we met in the shell of our new Society room. The scripture which came in course to be explained was, "Marvel not if the world hate you". We sang, "Arm of the Lord, awake, awake"!' One can almost see those shining, uplifted faces, as the little company stood on the bare boards in the stark simplicity of the place, undistracted and un-aided by their surroundings, oblivious of everything but the presence of the living God in their midst. The entry in the *Journal* ends with the words, 'And God, even our own God, gave us His blessing'.

The service marked another stage in the movement for which he was, humanly speaking, so largely responsible. It was certainly not his intention to erect buildings in opposition to those of the Church to which he belonged. He was forced by circum-stances to provide shelter for the Societies that wished to worship there. He could not see the outcome of these small beginnings.

The planning of the first building was probably influenced by Wesley's memories of the community buildings in the Moravian Settlement at Herrnhut. There was a long room, with forms and a desk cov-ered with green cloth. Two sconces, each holding eight candles, hung from the ceiling. Besides the main Society room there was a schoolroom where Wesley saw inquirers, a garret where he slept, and a stable for his horse. It was unpretentious, but it was hallowed by many prayers and great hope.

During the few days which remained of that first momentous visit to Bristol he continued to preach and to visit the Societies. He had to meet criticism, because some people who had heard him preach, had reacted strangely to the message. Patiently he dealt with each case, realizing differences of temperament and suspecting the more neurotic, until they 'grew out' of their convulsive manifestations into a calmer and more reasonable mind.

One of the preaching centres he had established was at Bath. It was then a most fashionable resort. All the 'quality' came there to take the waters. In the great Pump Room they gathered – a brilliant assembly, typical of the period.

At the entrance stood three busts, one of Pope, the poet, another of Sir Isaac Newton, the scientist, but in the centre, in the place of honour, a large one of Beau Nash. He was the uncrowned King of Bath, men said. On the brilliant crowd the stone figure looked down – the elegant dandy who dominated the situation. It was a condemnation of all their values.

There was, indeed, a superficiality about the culture of the age. Beneath the thin veneer which gave an appearance of polish, there lay a coarseness which was no better than the vulgarity of the inarticulate and hopeless mob.

More than one critic of Wesley has been content to judge him against the highly coloured pictures of the novelists, who have found a picturesque background for their gay adventurers. They have shown him as a sombre, self-righteous little figure spoiling sport without reason. Sometimes it is a healthy corrective to remember how shallow was the covering which gave a first impression of elegance and good taste. In point of fact, the quality were none too cleanly in their bodily habits nor their mental outlook, and beneath the glamour they were tragically weighed down by *taedium vitae* – that weariness of life which had burdened the Roman Empire in an earlier Augustan Age.

It is one thing to see the gaily-clad crowd of spectators at the Baths. Minstrels in the gallery are playing, and playing uncommonly well. Many of the fair ladies of the Court disport themselves in the water with the young gallants of the day. Conversation is sparkling; it is an age of repartee. When the hour or so is over, the bathers, wrapped in blankets, are carried back in sedan-chairs to their lodgings. Later they will spend the rest of the day at the card tables, gambling recklessly. It does look a gallant scene. It is most disconcerting to learn that they did not dream of changing the water in the bath more than once in two months!

To this superficial people John Wesley came with a message that reached men's hearts. It was unwelcome to Beau Nash and his cronies. They determined to end his pretensions and score off this pitiful little parson, so full of exhortations and admonitions. He was warned that if he dared to preach in the town he would have a hot reception. Such a warning made him the more determined to be there.

He found an unusually big crowd waiting. Rumour had been busy, and they were on tip-toe. The quality were eager to see the latest adventure of their idol. John Wesley began to preach, and astonished them by declaring that they were all alike, sinners – 'both high and low, rich and poor, one with another'. Whilst he was speaking a post-chaise, drawn by six grey horses, and accompanied by outriders, footmen, lackeys with French horns, stopped on the edge of the crowd. A man alighted with an air of studied elegance. The ruffles at his neck and wrists were of the most expensive lace; the heels of his crimson shoes were set with diamonds and brilliants; he doffed his monstrous white hat in greeting to the crowd. Was he not the King of Bath?

With seeming carelessness he sauntered towards the speaker. The crowd made way for him. The little man standing on a hillock went on, unmoved. 'By what authority do you preach, sir?' asked Beau Nash sarcastically. John stopped speaking, looked at him closely, then answered, 'By the authority of Jesus Christ, conveyed to me by the Archbishop of Canterbury, when he laid hands upon me and said "Take thou authority to preach the Gospel".' For a moment Beau Nash was surprised, then he said, 'This is contrary to Acts of Parliament, this is a conventicle'. Again John Wesley answered, 'Sir, the conventicles mentioned in that Act are seditious meetings: but this is not such; here is no shadow of sedition; for it is not contrary to the Act'. Beau Nash shuffled a little uneasily and bridled in his speech. He replied, 'I say it is, and besides your preaching frightens people out of their wits'. 'Sir, did you ever hear me preach?' asked Wesley. 'No.' 'How then can you judge what you have never heard?' 'Sir, by common report.' 'Common report is not enough. Give me leave, sir, to ask is not your name Nash?' 'My name is Nash.' 'Sir, I dare not judge of you by common report, I think it is not enough to judge by.' This was a severe blow, and Nash was staggered – the crowd knew the common report about Beau Nash! Then he stammered, 'I desire to know what these people come here for'.

At that, an old lady standing in the crowd piped out in her shrill voice, 'Sir, leave him to me; let an old woman answer him. You Mr. Nash take care of your body; we take care of our souls; and for the food of our souls we come here'. Beau Nash dropped his eyes, answered no word, just walked away. It was a strange and unexpected victory for this wandering preacher, aided by an old woman whose heart had been strangely warmed like his. The crowd melted away, and the coaches rolled off towards the Pump Room. A most disappointing afternoon!

So Wesley came to the end of his first visit to Bristol, and returned to London to settle certain difficulties in the Fetter Lane Society. In the great city there were still churches where he could preach. Field-preaching would surely be unnecessary here! The day after his return he went with Whitefield, who was still in London, to Blackheath. Twelve or fourteen thousand people had gathered to hear him preach. To Wesley's astonishment his friend insisted that he should deliver the sermon. He agreed, 'though nature recoiled', and he took his favourite subject, 'Jesus Christ, who of God is made unto us wisdom, righteousness, sanctification, and redemption'. Strangely enough his comment is, 'I was greatly moved with compassion for the rich that were there, to whom I made a particular application. Some of them seemed to attend, while others drove away their coaches from so uncouth a preacher'.

He had not forgotten the poor, silly idlers at Bath, so sure of their glamorous clothes, so tired of their aching hearts.

It was a busy week, but Sunday came at last. How would he use it? Where could he most surely preach?

There was a great open space at Upper Moorfields, the site of the modern Finsbury Square. To the south lay another piece of open ground, Middle Moorfields, and trees encircled both. It was a pleasant spot where Londoners took the air on Sundays, dressed in their best and in happy mood. Across Lower Moorfields, along the gravel walks, they came for their weekly promenade. But why were there seven thousand walking abroad at seven o'clock that Sunday morning? Why did they direct their steps to one particular place, instead of wandering idly to and fro? Why, if not to hear the little man who was standing on a wooden platform, announcing his text, 'Ho! every one that thirsteth, come ye to the waters'?

If you would hear him again that day you must cross London, walk through the outlying hamlet of Newington, until, a mile further on, you come to a great common at Kennington. It is a very different place. Here you will find the rag-tag and bobtail of London town. Here, on a week-day, you may see a cartful of criminals hanged. Here, sooner or later, you may come across all the pimps and procurers, the pickpockets and vagabonds, who haunt the darker streets of the city at nights. An unsavoury place. Here, that Sunday afternoon, at five or thereabouts, you will find fifteen thousand people listening eagerly, to that clear-voiced messenger who is saying, 'Look unto Me, and be ye saved, all ye ends of the earth'. There is no menace in his words, no wild condemnation in his careful sentences. He is a voice, uttering the urgent invitation of his Master. The crowd know sincerity when they see and hear it. He would not last five minutes on Kennington Common if he were a charlatan, or if he were conducting experiments on the raw material of their souls for the sake of his own! They are not driven mad by a ferocious onslaught of words. For the first time in their lives they dare to wonder if God cares.

So London heard the man who had made up his mind that the world was to be his parish. Little room in the Horsefair, brick-yard or pit-head, stone steps in Gracious Street, Moorfields or Kennington Common – it was all one to him. He is going to those who need him – and first to those who need him most. Never again will he know a settled home. His journeys are beginning according to plan. Up and down the land he must range. His bases, for bases there must be, will be established in London, Bristol and, later, in Newcastle.

The winter of 1739–40 was very cold. The need for some shelter for the crowds was becoming desperate. The last thing in his mind was to erect buildings that should rival the Anglican churches, but something must surely be done if the work of field-preaching was to be consolidated. There must be shelters for the little bands who were growing rapidly, and there must be some linking up and ordering of scattered communities.

One day, two men, whom he did not know, came to Wesley and suggested that he should preach in an old ruined building near Moorfields. It was called the Foundery, and it stood on Windmill Hill. For many years it had been an arsenal, until in 1716, whilst the guns, taken from the French in Marlborough's campaigns, were being recast, a tragic accident happened. An explosion shattered the building, killed many of the workmen and caused the Royal Arsenal to be moved from Windmill Hill to Woolwich.

The building was bought for one hundred and fifteen pounds, and on Sunday, November 11, 1739, John Wesley preached to several thousand people standing amidst the vast, uncouth heap of ruins. On that day, the eleventh of November, he proclaimed the spiritual armistice on which the peace of men and nations must, at last, be founded.

Another seven hundred pounds had to be raised, partly on loan, to recondition the building. It became the first Methodist Chapel in London, and a little later suitable premises were added. There were two front doors, one for the chapel and one for the preacher's house, the school and the band-room. There was a bell hung in a very plain belfry. Every morning at five o'clock it summoned the people to early service, and every evening at nine they came there for family worship. One can imagine them, although it was only two hundred years ago, wandering along those dark lanes, the flickering candles in their horn lanterns guiding them through the early morning darkness to this simple House of God. There were no pews, just plain seats, most of them without backs. Under the front gallery were three rows for women and under the side gallery three for men. The front gallery was occupied by women, the side gallery by men. Perhaps the best description is one that Wesley gives: 'From the beginning the men and women sat apart, as they always did in the primitive Church; none were suffered to call any place their own, but the first comer sat down first. They had no pews; and all the benches for rich and poor were of the same construction.' In the band-room which was about eighty feet by twenty feet classes met, a day-school was held, and at one end there was the book-room where Wesley's tracts and various writings were sold to the congregation. Over this band-room were smaller rooms which Wesley himself used when he was in London. In one of them, his mother, Susanna, died. Beyond these buildings was the coach-house and stable.

The old pulpit, which Wesley first used in the Foundery, now stands in the beautiful Chapel of Richmond College. One remembers experiencing a twinge of disappointment at discovering it was made of rough deal and elm. The feeling was momentary. No rare timber would have been so fitting. It was a field-preacher's pulpit after all!

Here then, in the old Foundery, Wesley had his first London pulpit. Here in this gaunt bare room these Methodist pioneers knelt in lowliness of spirit, and knew the joy of God's pardoning grace.

The third permanent centre was established at Newcastle. In 1742 Wesley decided to go northward on a preaching tour. Towards the end of May he rode with John Taylor, into Gateshead, where he stayed in a little inn at the old bridge-head. Next day he went into Newcastle and was appalled at the condition of the people. 'So much drunkenness, cursing and swearing (even from the mouths of little children), do I never remember to have seen and heard before.' How they needed his Master! That was always his reaction to such a situation. Early on Sunday morning he and John Taylor stood in Sand-gate, the poorest part of the town, and sang the hundredth Psalm. A crowd began to collect. Out of Wesley's pocket came the little Bible, and in a moment he was preaching, to those broken, battered folk, about Him who was wounded, too, but for the sins of men. When he finished the crowd did not disperse. The message and the messenger had amazed them. They looked at the spare figure and won-dered. Then they heard him speaking again: 'If you desire to know who I am, my name is John Wesley. At five in the evening, with God's help, I design to preach again.' True to his promise he came to Sand-gate to find, this time, a tremendous crowd waiting. They heard him eagerly, and clutched his coat, beg-ging him to stay with them. It was not the reception one would expect of a man who has been portrayed as frightening people into the madhouse!

Unfortunately he had promised to travel back to Bristol by Tuesday night. Charles Wesley rode north as soon as he could, and Newcastle received him with great joy. When John returned he bought land near

Pilgrim Street Gate. On December 20, 1742, the foundation-stone of the 'House' was laid, and three months later he preached in the partly finished building. When it was completed the lower part was used as a chapel, fitted with pulpit and forms. Over the main building was a band-room, and class-rooms. On the upper story were apartments for the preachers and their families, and on the roof itself was a wooden hut, eleven feet square, which was called 'Mr. Wesley's study'.

If we draw a line between Bristol and London, another between London and Newcastle and a third between Newcastle and Bristol, we shall have a rough outline of Wesley's travel routes. At these three centres he now had permanent buildings as the headquarters of the Societies there.

Meanwhile an even more important process of building had been begun. The little spiritual communities known as 'bands' must be linked up and ordered, so that there was some sense of corporate life and fellowship. It would be useless to continue to hold great mass assemblies, where people entered into the primary experience of conversion, and to ride off leaving them alone and uninstructed. They were encouraged to join together in little groups.

After a while he discovered ways in which he might improve the first elementary methods. In 1739 many little Societies began to be formed in London. There were only three or four people in them at first, but they were modelled rather on the lines of the Religious Societies already existing. These bands, for which, in 1738, Wesley had first made the rules, met every week. There were not less than five or more than ten people in them, and they were the inner circle of the Methodist Societies. Later on the Class-Meeting was developed, and in addition Lovefeasts and Watch-night Services were held. The whole point in Wesley's mind was how to hold together the people who were beginning to share a common experience of the Risen Christ in their hearts. Leaders were appointed for the Classes, which were held in all sorts of places, in farm kitchens, in little cottage parlours, in elaborate drawing-rooms; sometimes they even met in a coal-mine, and very often in a barn. Leaders kept the names of members in a little book, and every quarter each member received a ticket of membership.

Another very strong influence, which held together these little Societies, was the singing of the new hymns which were written by Charles Wesley or translated by John. Although Samuel Wesley, the old Rector of Epworth, had been something of a poet, and John and Charles could write rhyming verse, it was only after 1738, and the great awakening of Charles, that he began to write his marvellous hymns. Within a year he had written, 'Where shall my wondering soul begin?' 'And can it be that I should gain', 'Come, Holy

Ghost, all-quickening fire!' Next year he wrote, 'Christ, whose glory fills the skies' and 'Jesu, Lover of my soul', 'O for a thousand tongues to sing', and 'Earth, rejoice, our Lord is King'. Such hymns as these immediately welded together the people who were singing them, just as a little later the 'Marseillaise' united the French people. No one can understand the real meaning of Methodism who is not prepared to read carefully the hymns of Charles Wesley and to try to understand their vital message to an eighteenth-century England, whose religious outlook had become dim and impersonal.

There had been no hymn-singing, as we understand it, in the Church of England. The Psalms, which had been arranged by Tate and Brady or Sternhold and Hopkins, were sometimes sung, but they never produced enthusiastic congregational singing. In 1696 there had been hymn-books issued by the Congregationalists whose great hymn-writers were Philip Doddridge and Dr. Watts. In 1737 John Wesley had published a little book of translations for his people in Georgia. He had evidently got the idea from the Moravians, who were great singers, but it was not till Charles Wesley became the hymn-writer of Methodism that their full value was realized. They are not just solemn paraphrases of scripture – they have their own vitality, they are alive, your heart dances as you sing, or it is bowed with shame, or again it rises up on wings to the very throne of

God. They are not pieces of patchwork, there are no unnecessary adjectives, no catch-phrases; some of the hymns remind us of the poetry of William Blake, and some are like the battle-cry of the Scottish clans.

Gradually, then, the little communities were built together in their common, progressive experience. There was no question of calling them one Church, though perhaps some of the clergy began to have their fears.

The work did not go unopposed. Pamphleteers wrote scurrilous criticisms, and some of the most cultured of the clergy made John Wesley's task more difficult. But his heart was burning. He could not be stopped by acid comments or by criticisms that caricatured, not only his brave little body, but his fearless and confident message. Neither stones from the mob nor vitriolic outbursts of the lampooners could turn him back. One of the critics came to George Whitefield and said, 'Sir, do you think when we get to heaven we shall see John Wesley?' 'No, sir', answered George Whitefield, 'I fear not, for he will be so near the Eternal Throne and we shall be at such a distance, we shall hardly get a sight of him.'

CHAPTER 8

THE OPEN ROAD

'I LOOK upon the whole world as my parish', said John Wesley, and he certainly tried to cover that portion of his parish which was England as often as he could. He was dependent on a horse for fifty years, and the various horses that he rode were, in turn, dependent on muddy lanes and broken turnpike roads that would dismay us to-day.

The road from Windsor to Petworth was only forty miles long, but it took fourteen hours to travel over it. 'Almost every mile', said Hervey, 'was signalized by the overturn of the carriage or its temporary swamping in the mire. Even the royal chariot would have fared no better than the rest had it not been for the relays of peasants, who poised and kept it erect by the strength of arm and shouldered forward the last nine miles, in which tedious operation six good hours were consumed.'

When the roads fell into disrepair loose stones tumbled into the holes and traffic bumped and rumbled along once more. Ruts were often so deep that the horses could not stand up in them, and in these great holes water was almost always standing.

In the reign of George II it was said, 'The road

between Kensington and London is grown so infinitely bad that we live here in the same solitude as we would do if cast on a rock in the middle of the ocean; and all the Londoners tell us that there is between them and us an impassable gulf of mud'.

From London to Oxford, there were many narrow places where a horse could not pass a carriage, and the stones which had been used to fill up the holes were so large as to risk breaking the horse's neck.

In *A Six Months' Tour Through the North of England* written in 1770, the Lancashire Road from Preston to Wigan is described. 'You will here meet with ruts which I actually measured four feet deep, and floating with mud only from the wet summer; what therefore must it be after the winter?'

Daniel Defoe has rather an amusing passage about his tour in Sussex, in 1724. He writes: 'Going to church at a country village, not far from Lewes, I saw an ancient lady – and a lady of very good quality I assure you – drawn to church in her coach with six oxen, nor was it done in frolic or humour, but mere necessity, the way being so stiff and deep that no horse could go in it.'

Along such roads John Wesley journeyed on his horse, not slowly or leisurely but eagerly for he was a messenger of the King. Five or six times in each day's journey he would stop at a village green, or some other convenient place, and preach to the people. In between these services, as he rode, he would read books. Apparently he had learned to trust his horse implicitly and broke all the rules of horsemanship by letting it have its head. Occasionally he was thrown, but seldom came to serious grief.

He talked with many of his fellow travellers as he had opportunity. Wagons lumbered along and he rode past them with a word to the wagoner. Long strings of pack-horses went from town to town, carrying cloth or coals or some other commodity. The quickest way to get perishable goods, fish from the coast or vegetables from the field or meat from the market-town, was on pack-horses. Great herds of sheep and cattle used the same roads and there were other less peaceful travellers. Highwaymen were constantly making their raids on those whom they thought they could rob to advantage.

It is said that John Wesley was stopped by a highwayman who demanded his money or his life. He gave him what money he had but with the gift he offered some advice. 'Let me speak one word to you,' he said. 'The time may come when you will regret this course of life. Remember this, the blood of Iesus Christ cleanseth from all sin.' Years afterwards a stranger came up to him, after he had been preaching, and asked if he remembered the incident. 'I was the man who stopped you', said the stranger, 'and that verse you quoted was the means of changing my life and habits.' The story may be apocryphal, but somehow I do not think that John Wesley started in his saddle when he heard a rustling in the hedge or even when he wondered if he would see a masked figure riding up to his side with a horse-pistol held at his head. When danger threatened he did not consider its effect on him – he was always so busy in devising ways of getting his message home to the people whom he met. The knight had ridden far since he feared the storm aboard the *Simmonds*.

Another day, as he rode along through Newport Pagnell, he overtook a man who seemed anxious for conversation. John Wesley put away his book in his saddle-bag, and began to talk to him. As they rode the man began to argue about religious affairs. In vain John Wesley tried to avoid the contentious subject, the man grew excited, and said he believed John Wesley was rotten at heart, and supposed he was one of John Wesley's followers. He answered, 'No, I am John Wesley himself'. Upon this he appeared as one who unawares had trodden on a snake, and 'would gladly have run away outright, but being the better mounted of the two I kept close to his side, and endeavoured to show him his heart until we came into the street of Northampton'. It must have been a wonderful sight for the people of the town as they saw these two horsemen, the one pursuing the other, and telling him, as he would have put it, 'good and plain' his errors.

Nor was all his journeying by road – he must

cross fords, he must take ship to Ireland. When the roads were so bad that his horse could not keep its feet, he must tramp alone across the moors. Once, on his way to Grimsby, the river Trent was in flood and a raging storm prevented the boatmen putting him across. He begged them to make the attempt lest he should disappoint the congregation at Grimsby. Yielding to pressure they put off with six men, two women and three horses in the boat. Suddenly the boat heeled over, horses and men being thrown in a heap. The boatmen strained at the oars, the horses leaped overboard, but at last the boat reached the farther bank. Everyone got ashore, save John Wesley, who lay pinned to the bottom of the boat by a crowbar which had run through the string of his boot, so that he must have perished had the vessel capsized. But the congregation at Grimsby were not disappointed!

He very rarely took a long way round because the short way was dangerous. In February 1748 he had to wait at Holyhead because the weather was unfavourable. He became impatient with the sailors. 'I never knew men make such poor, lame excuses as these bumpkins did for not sailing. It put me in mind of the epigram,

> There are, if rightly I may think
> Five causes why a man should drink,

which with a little alteration would just suit them.

There are, unless my memory fail,
Five causes why we should not sail;
The fog is thick, the wind is high;
It rains, or may do by and by;
Or – any other reason why.'

No storms ever turned him back. In February 1740 he rode to Newcastle. It was a wild winter but nothing daunted him. 'Many a rough journey have I had before, but none like this I ever had; between wind, and hail, and rain, and ice, and snow, and driving sleet, and piercing wind. But it is past, those days will return no more, and are therefore as though they had never been.'

Healthy though riding in the open air was, there always seems to have been a sense of tremendous urgency about the Knight of the Burning Heart. He never had time to waste, he was full of observation as he rode along, but an easy-going man never found him companionable. That was why Dr. Johnson, who would have loved to talk to him, said, 'John Wesley's conversation is good, but he is never at leisure, he is always obliged to go at a certain hour. This is very disagreeable to a man who loves to cross his legs and have his talk out, as I do'.

Many of the chairs which are still treasured because he used them are so shaped that he could sit astraddle as he talked. There is one kept in the vestry at City Road which has a desk on the back so that, as he sat facing it, he could write.

He had no sympathy with those who allowed weather to prevent worship! His religion was of such importance as to dominate all the forces of nature. One Saturday evening when he was preaching at North Shields one of the young women, in what we should call the choir, stayed at home because of a snow-storm. He saw her on Monday evening, and putting his hand on her shoulder said quietly, 'So miss, you were afraid of the snow?' She didn't answer but she appeared at the service in the chapel next evening, thinking he had finished reproving her. Quite quietly, however, he gave out his text from Proverbs xxxi. 21, 'She is not afraid of the snow'.

In December 1765 his horse threw him, and he was hurt much more than he had been by any previous misadventure. A lady, called Miss Lewen of Leytonstone, gave him a chaise and a pair of horses in order that he might journey in safety but he could go much better on horse-back, and it was not till later in life that he really reconciled himself to travelling by carriage. Even then he fitted the carriage with bookshelves, so that it would be a travelling study.

Time and again when his life seemed in peril he quietly prayed and ceased to worry. Once the vessel in which he was sailing grounded on the rocks at Holyhead, and the captain was in despair. 'We immediately went to prayer', said John Wesley, 'and presently the ship, I know not how, shot off the rocks and pursued her way without any more damage.'

Even as an old man his good humour did not fail him, and it was one of the travelling mercies for his companions. He was riding with Joseph Entwisle when Joseph's horse stumbled and pitched him right over its head. Fortunately he alighted on his feet. John Wesley said smiling, 'Well done, Joseph. I could not have done better than that myself'. So he rode along with the light heart of a troubadour and the courage of a knight errant. Even the greyness of his clothes, his horse, and the roads themselves did not rob life of its colour for him. It was a blithesome pilgrimage which had ceased to be a selfish journey. Everywhere he went he brought gifts above money and above price to the people by the wayside or in the market-place, on shipboard or in the town.

CHAPTER 9

THE KNIGHT RIDES ON

THERE were several reasons why the mobs began to treat John Wesley roughly. The people did not understand what he was seeking for them or what he had found for himself. Opposition sprang up in town and country.

Sometimes it was the result of an alliance between the local parson and the squire, both of whom imagined that the Methodists were 'levellers'. As the Duchess of Buckingham wrote to the Countess of Huntingdon, 'It is monstrous to be told that you have a heart as sinful as the common wretches that crawl on the earth. This is highly offensive and insulting; and I cannot but wonder that your Lady-ship should relish any sentiment so much at variance with high life and good breeding'.

At other times it was stupidly rumoured that Wesley was a supporter of the Young Pretender, and therefore a Roman Catholic and a friend of the French. The mob was not slow to seize upon him as a spy and to discover a new sport in baiting the Methodists.

There were, however, a few who felt a real concern about the heretics and enthusiasts who were disturbing the normal course of their religious life.

To some sincere clergy John Wesley appeared to be a rebel preacher, who treated things that were important to them with no respect at all. He, himself, had found it most difficult, at first, to recognize the functions of the lay-preachers, and when he accepted laymen as co-workers in the preaching of the Gospel, they were shocked and enraged.

Bull-baiting was a favourite sport and the mob suddenly discovered a pleasant variation. They would plague the bull till he turned upon the Methodists.

So it happened one day as John rode into Pensford, he dismounted by the village green and began to preach. Scarcely had he begun, when a mob, paid for its pains, came charging down on him. They were driving a bull, already maddened by fierce blows and the hideous din, goading it on till they steered it towards the preacher. But the beast was wiser than its drivers: time and time again it swerved to right or left of the little man who stood bareheaded, singing a hymn and sometimes praying quietly. A group of people who had invited him to come, stood round him – afraid but very steady!

The mob was exasperated. The bull was tired. A dozen dogs snapped at its heels, a score of boys prodded it with sharp sticks. The rabble thrust at it, urging it towards the wooden table on which the preacher stood. He did not flinch. The beast was very near. He reached down his hand, and turned the shaggy, blood-stained head aside. The poor brute passed by, but the mob, roaring in vexation, surged towards the little table. Just as it toppled over, the faithful body-guard bore John Wesley away on their shoulders.

For a moment or two the rabble spent its rage on smashing the table to bits; then they turned to find the preacher. He was standing, close by, finishing his sermon. Like whipped dogs they slunk away a little distance, then sat down to listen!

It did not always end like that. One Sunday, later in the same year, John walked out to preach on Coverlet Fields, near Whitechapel Road. Thousands of people came to hear him. Most of them listened eagerly, but a few hooligans rounded up a herd of cows, and tried to drive them into the crowd. The cattle were obstinate and ran away. Sport was being spoiled. The disappointed men seized stones and hurled them at the preacher. They roared with delight as he was hit, but suddenly fell silent. He was badly cut. 'One of the stones struck me just between the eyes: but I felt no pain at all; and, when I wiped away the blood, went on testifying with a loud voice that God had given to them that believed not the spirit of fear but of power, and of love, and of a sound mind. And, by the spirit which now appears to the whole congregation I plainly saw what a blessing it is when it is given us even in the lowest degree to suffer for His Name's sake.' There is no word of complaint in his description. He rather pities the people who were tormenting him.

Persecution did not dismay him. His tormentors were more troubled than he. Sometimes they amused him, sometimes they forced him to righteous indignation, but they never made him surrender.

Once, at Bedford, two or three men continued to interrupt his sermon by shouting. One of them had filled his pockets with rotten eggs to throw at the preacher. A friendly soul in the audience noticed it, stole up quietly behind the interrupter, clapped his hands on the bulging pockets and smashed the eggs. John Wesley wrote in his *Journal* with boyish glee: 'In an instant he was perfumed all over, though it was not so sweet as balsam.'

The most serious and, perhaps, most famous of the riots happened in 1743 in Staffordshire. The ancient footway ran across heath-covered commons honeycombed with rabbit warrens. Here, on holidays, great crowds assembled for the bull-baiting and the cock-fighting which was their chief amusement. The agricultural labourer, unable to read or write, toiled all day in the fields, ate frugal meals of rye bread and cheese, or potatoes, and in the evening sat somnolent or drunk in the village ale-house. The squire seldom travelled far afield, but lived and died in the parish where he was born, as illiterate as the peasants who tilled his fields. Bewigged, he rode out in his long coat with silver buttons to the tavern where he drank heavily, then mounted his horse to leap five-barred gates with the abandon of a schoolboy and a complete disregard of his standing corn. On Sundays he snored heavily in the dismal church, and coming home sat on an uncomfortable settle, drowsing.

In such a dull world the 'cockings' at Wednesbury or the bull-baiting at High Bullen were welcome interludes. No wonder that the baiting of the Methodists was popular. It was an extra holiday and cost nothing.

At first Wednesbury received the Methodist preachers kindly. Both Charles and John Wesley gathered numbers of the townspeople into 'societies'. Then disaster came. Tactless preachers arrived, and criticized the clergy. Feuds sprang up. The local vicar, originally friendly and helpful, was now indignant. The more unruly elements got out of hand, windows were smashed and houses raided. It was the first time the members of the little society had realized the price they might have to pay for their loyalty. They did not waver. Spasmodic outbursts were followed by more organized attacks. The vicar and some of the magistrates began to take a hand. A proclamation was issued. It was a pompous and ridiculous document: 'Whereas we, his Majesty's Justices of the Peace for the said County of Stafford, have received information that several disorderly persons, styling themselves Methodist Preachers, go about raising routs and riots, to the great damage of

His Majesty's people. . . .' The few scattered folk sat behind their broken windows, amidst the debris of their homes, and waited to be arrested for their 'unlawful doings'.

Word was brought to John Wesley at Birmingham. Immediately he rode out to see for himself. On October 20, 1743, he came to the town. At noon he dismounted in High Bullen, climbed a horseback, near the malthouse, and began to preach. 'Jesus Christ, the same yesterday, and to-day, and for ever.' He read the words from the little Bible and began to expound them. The crowd listened in silence; not a hand was raised nor a stone thrown. 'The Lord fought for us, and we held our peace.' A difficult beginning if Justices Lane and Persehouse are to impound him for 'unlawful doings'.

In the afternoon he sat quietly writing at Francis Ward's. Suddenly he heard shouting in the street. Through the window he saw a mob gathering outside the house. He laid down his pen, fell on his knees and 'prayed that God would disperse them, and it was so. One went this way, and another that; so that, in half an hour, not a man was left'. By five o'clock they had come back again. 'Bring out the minister', they cried. 'We will have the minister.' 'Bring in your leader' was Wesley's answer. A great strapping fellow came noisily into the quiet room. John spoke to him for a minute or so, and the lion had become a lamb. 'Go and bring some more ot your friends to me – the angriest you can find.' The man went obediently, and returned in a moment with two others 'ready to swallow the ground with rage'. In two minutes they were as calm as their leader.

John got up and went out to the great crowd gathered in the street. 'Bring me a chair', he said. 'Now, what do any of you want with me?' 'We want you to go with us to the Justice', they shouted, expecting him to refuse. 'That I will', said John, 'with all my heart.' Before he got down from his chair, however, he spoke a few words 'which God applied'. The crowd was astonished and impressed. 'The gentleman is an honest gentleman', they said, 'and we will spill our blood in his defence.'

'Shall we go to the Justice to-night or in the morning?' asked John as though it was a pleasure not to be deferred. 'To-night, to-night', cried the mob accommodatingly.

Quite calmly he set off with two or three hundred following him.

They had gone no more than a mile when night fell, and with the darkness came a heavy storm of rain. The magistrate, Mr. Lane, lived at Bentley Hall, about two miles from Wednesbury. Some of the mob ran on ahead to tell him they were bringing the preacher. 'What have I to with Mr. Wesley?' he shouted. 'Go and carry him back again.' The door slammed but in a few moments the whole crowd arrived, shouting and banging the gate. A servant came out to tell them Mr. Lane was in bed. They wouldn't listen to him. The son of the magistrate appeared and asked them what was the matter. Some one shouted, 'Why, an't please you, they sing Psalms all day; ay, and make folks rise at five in the morning. And what would your Worship advise us to do?' 'Go home and be quiet,' was the reply.

It rather staggered the mob. They would get no satisfaction from Mr. Lane, so they decided to go on to Justice Persehouse who lived at Walsall. When they got there the Justice sent word that he was in bed. They were nonplussed. What should they do next? Just as they had decided to take John back, a new mob coming from Walsall met them. In a moment there was a free fight. The newcomers were fresh and eager for 'sport'. The rest ran away. Shouting and hustling they bore their prisoner back to town. Twice he tried to slip out of their hands, and find refuge in a house as they passed. Once a man grabbed him by the hair and pulled him out of the doorway. Once the householder thrust him away, lest the mob pull his house about his ears. John stood fast on the threshold. 'Are you willing to hear me speak?' he shouted, but the mob screamed back, 'no, no, knock his brains out; down with him; kill him at once'. A few answered them, 'Nay, let's hear him first'.

When they ceased to shout, being out of breath,

John spoke very calmly. 'What evil have I done? Which of you all have I wronged in word or deed?' He tried to make them hear, but his voice broke under the strain. 'Bring him away! Bring him away,' howled the mob. His voice came back and he prayed aloud. Something happened – not to the mob but in the heart of their leader. He called to the little man praying on the doorstep. 'Sir, I will spend my life for you: follow me, and not one soul here shall touch a hair of your head.' The shop-keeper regained his courage and cried out, 'Shame on you, let him go'. A butcher standing near took up the cry, and laying about him, stopped four or five who rushed fiercely towards Wesley. The people fell back. The leader and his companions closed round John and bore him safely through the crowd. They followed muttering and angry. On the bridge they grew more threatening, but the bodyguard clambered round the mill-dam, hurried through the meadows, and brought their man, by God's help, safe to Wednesbury. He had lost nothing, save a flap of his waistcoat and a little skin from one of his hands.

It was a wonderful deliverance. When he got back to Francis Ward's, he found many people praying for him. They welcomed him as one risen from the dead, and, indeed, he might well have died that night. Once they had tried to trip him on the steep, slippery hill, but he kept his feet or he would surely have been kicked to death. Clutching hands had striven to tear his clothes from his back, but they could not get a hold. One man had torn the flap of a pocket off but it was the wrong one. The only banknote he had was in the other pocket! Several times a man beat him with a great oak stick. 'If he had struck me once on the back part of my head, it would have saved him all farther trouble.' Another came rushing at him, with arm raised to strike, but suddenly let drop his club and stroked John's head, crying, 'What soft hair he has!'

How did it all happen? It is a stark, straight story of an angry mob, incessantly on the move, on a dark, wet night. One may hazard a guess at hypnotic influences when one thinks of a congregation gathered in a lighted hall, listening to an impassioned orator, but here are enraged people, out for sport, drenched with rain, baulked of their prey in the darkness. Here, too, is a prizefighter from the bear-garden, depending for his livelihood on providing the mob with sensation and rough horse-play, suddenly snatching from his patrons the very thing he has set out to provide.

There is heroism in the happenings that night. All through the adventure a little group fought their way to his side whenever they could – William Fitch, Edward Slater, John Griffiths, and Joan Parks. Yet in the last issue it was no human hand which changed the heart of the grim old bruiser and his boon companions so that they risked the vengeance of the rabble to deliver the man they had come to bait. In the darkness John had stumbled on beneath a shower of blows, his face and mouth battered and bleeding but feeling, as he says, 'no more pain than if they had touched me with a straw'. There were more forces at work in the darkness than can be analysed in a laboratory or defined in a book! They were forces so wonderful that, as he looked on them, he said, 'By how gentle degrees does God prepare us for His will!'

In the morning he got up, mounted his horse not stealthily but quite openly, and rode on his way to Nottingham. Every one he passed called out affectionately to him. In the afternoon Charles met him. 'My brother came, delivered out of the mouth of the lion. He looked like a soldier of Christ; his clothes were torn to tatters. . . . But his work is not finished.' He had come to Nottingham to preach the Gospel, not to mend his clothes or lick his wounds. The light of the next battle is already in his face.

Mobs are often more difficult to fight than armies. They have no tactics and are for ever doing the unexpected. He discovered one way of defeating them – he always looked a mob in the face. Time and again they came like a great wave rolling towards him, but he looked straight at them, spoke quietly, and presently the wave rolled back. Sometimes individuals, spurred on by the fury of the mob, or by the hope of reward or favour from the local clergyman or squire, came to arrest him. Almost always they went away without him, muttering some paltry excuse.

In 1745, when all England was agog because of the rumoured coming of the Pretender, gossip had it that John Wesley was a Jacobite, if not a Jesuit. The press-gang was busily recruiting men, and it was easy to use its powers to remove undesirables from a district and to press them into His Majesty's Navy. More than one attempt was made to get rid of Wesley and his preachers by this method.

In midsummer he rode west, coming presently to the great pit at Gwennap. In the amphitheatre the crowd was just settling down on the grassy banks to listen to him, when two horsemen came riding furiously, followed by a *posse* of men. They spurred their horses into the crowd to seize such likely fellows as might be there, fit for the King's ships. The people began to sing a hymn, perhaps a little defiantly. The horsemen were exasperated. One of them, Francis Beauchamp, afterwards Sheriff of Cornwall, looked at Wesley and shouted, 'Seize him, seize him! I say seize the preacher for His Majesty's service!' Not a man stirred. Beside himself with rage, he struck wildly at his servants, cursing them the while. Still no one moved to do his bidding. He leaped from his horse, snatched at Wesley's cassock, and cried out, 'I take you to serve His Majesty'. Without a word of protest John Wesley turned and went with him.

This was not quite what Mr. Beauchamp had

expected. Suddenly he found himself walking arm-in-arm with the man he had come to arrest. They tramped on for three-quarters of a mile, while he raged about the wickedness of the Methodists. When he had spent himself, John Wesley said with deadly quiet voice, 'Sir, be they what they will I apprehend it will not justify you seizing me in this manner and violently carrying me away, as you said, to serve His Majesty'. This was a new aspect of the situation, and Beauchamp replied, 'I seize you! And violently carry you away! No, sir; no. Nothing like it. I asked you to go with me to my house, and you said you was willing; and if so, you are welcome; and if not, you are welcome to go when you please'.

There is a touch of Nelson's strategy about John's answer. He is going to carry the partial victory to a finish. 'Sir', he said, innocently, 'I know not if it would be safe for me to go back through this rabble.' 'Sir,' said Mr. Beauchamp, 'I will go with you myself.' So the man who had come to arrest him, walked back as his escort, protecting him to Gwennap!

Two days later John Wesley rode to Falmouth to visit a member who was ill. As soon as he dismounted and went into the house a huge crowd of people gathered. It was almost like a siege. The lady of the house and her daughter tried to quieten them but it was no use. The mob roared, 'Bring out the Canorum. Where is the Canorum?' (This strange

Cornish word means singer, and was probably given to the Methodists because of their fondness for hymn-singing.) John Wesley and his friends inside made no reply. The mob burst in the outer door, and filled up the passage. There was only a thin partition between them. For once he decided to suffer a siege. The mistress of the house and her daughter had escaped. He was left, with a frightened servant girl, to meet the mob. Carefully he took down a large looking-glass which hung against the little partition. It must not be broken!

'Oh, sir, what must we do?' said the terrified girl as she heard the clamour of the crowd outside.

'We must pray, my child,' he said calmly.

'But, sir, is it not better for you to hide yourself?' she asked, and pointed to a cupboard.

'No, it is best for me to stand just where I am,' he answered.

The fury of the crowd increased. Sailors, from the privateers just come into harbour, pushed their way through, determined to see the fun. They set their shoulders to the door, crying, 'Avast, lads, avast'. The hinges groaned, and the door fell with a crash.

Before the sailors could regain their balance John stepped into their midst. 'Here I am,' he answered sharply. 'Which of you has anything to say to me? To which of you have I done any wrong? To you, or to you, or you?' They fell back, like schoolboys, shamefaced. And so he came through the midst, bareheaded, into the street.

The crowd gaped. He raised his voice and said loudly, 'Neighbours, countrymen, do you desire to hear me speak?' In a moment the crowd swayed. 'Yes, yes, he shall speak, he shall, nobody shall hinder him.' He looked round for a chair or a stool on which he might stand. The crowd hemmed him in. He raised his voice, and shouted. As far as the sound carried, the people were hushed and still. Some of the leaders swore not a man should touch him. A clergyman and two or three other gentlemen surrounded him, and he walked with them to the house of Mrs. Maddern. The crowd had followed, and now stood sullenly before the door.

He would like to have mounted his horse and ridden off, but his friends feared for his life. They led him through the house to the back entrance, across the little garden, beyond the gate to the edge of the sea. In a moment they had bundled him into a boat and were rowing him to Penryn. The mob saw they had been cheated, and ran cursing and threatening along the shore. When the boat reached the landing-place, John clambered out, strode up the steep, narrow passage from the sea, and walked calmly through the waiting crowd. The leader stepped towards him. He looked him straight in the face and said, 'I wish you a good night'. The man did not speak; he stood motionless. No rapier could have transfixed him so completely. As he waited, silently staring, John walked towards the horse that had been brought, put his foot in the stirrup, mounted and rode away. 'I wish you a good night.' The words had only slowly reached the man's brain. Suddenly he began to curse, but the only answer was the clatter of hoofs in the distance.

So through the years of persecution, the Knight of the Burning Heart rode without fear and without serious hurt. Even the armour of an Achilles or a Lancelot was not invulnerable, but John Wesley, with his old riding coat and the little Bible, rode safely, clad in armour not made with hands, which no weapon forged on earth could pierce.

Often, in the heat of attack, men saw how stupid their anger had been. Turning, they faced the mob which, the moment before, they had been urging to the attack. Many a day a leader became his body-guard.

His own reaction to this time of stress is faithfully recorded in the *Journal*. His comments are always full of gratitude to God for his deliverance. There is never any arrogance, and seldom any criticism of the sheep who posed as wolves! It was a triumphal progress – not of John Wesley but of his Master. After the riot at Falmouth he wrote: 'Though the hands of perhaps some hundreds of people were lifted up to strike or throw, they were one and all stopped in the mid-way, so that not a man touched me with one of his fingers. Neither was anything thrown from first to last, so that I had not even a speck of dust on my clothes.'

The years rolled on. He was white-haired, shrunken in body a little, but brave as a lion still. He rode into Falmouth, forty years after the riot, and said, 'The last time I was here I was taken prisoner by an immense mob, groping and roaring like lions. But how is the tide turned! High and low now lined the streets from one end of the town to the other, out of stark love and kindness, gaping and staring as if the King were going by'. And so the King was, in the heart of His servant John Wesley.

CHAPTER 10

HE CHANGED ENGLAND

Wʜᴇɴ Augustine Birrell was visiting Cornwall he said to a miner, 'You seem a very temperate people here. How did it happen?' The old Cornishman bared his head, and as if he were looking into the distant past, said quietly, 'There came a man amongst us, and his name was John Wesley'.

There have been other men whose advent has changed the life and manners of a community, but there have been few whose advantages seemed so small and whose influence was so profound. He was always poor; he began his real work as a clergyman with no official cure of souls, and he began his preaching when almost all the pulpits in the land were barred against him. As Birrell concludes a survey of his life he writes: 'No man lived nearer the centre than John Wesley, neither Clive nor Pitt, neither Mansfield nor Johnson. You cannot cut him out of our national life. No single figure influenced so many minds, no single voice touched so many hearts. No other man did such a life's work for England.'

The creation of what is called Methodism was perhaps the least of the major results of his life. In a terse sentence, Dr. Fitchett summarizes the issue.

'He restored Christianity to its place as a living force in the personal creed of men and in the life of the nation.'

He effected this change not because he brought some new theological theory, nor because he devised modern ecclesiastical machinery, nor even because he spoke with persuasive eloquence and hypnotic power. The beginning of the transformation was in his own heart and its end no man can know. He interpreted his own experience with such passionate sincerity that the wayfaring man understood and responded. Heart after heart was kindled into flame; mind after mind was convinced of a new reality; one after another the solitary, hopeless folk felt the touch of God upon their lives and began to live. 'England escaped a political revolution because she had undergone a spiritual revolution,' but the spiritual revolution of the nation was begun by the man whose heart, being strangely warmed, strove to share its secret with volcanic urgency. The middle and lower classes were fired with new enthusiasm born of the tremendous conviction that God cared and that they, voteless and voiceless in the national life, were yet included in the eternal purposes of God.

The transformation of the individual affected his relationship to his fellows and changed his attitude to society. It altered his mental outlook and wakened his conscience to a new sense of right and wrong. All these stages – personal, social, intellectual, and moral – were the result of a spiritual experience. The revolution in the hearts of individuals spread so that presently there was a new sense of the sacredness of personality, a new conception of the possibilities of service, in short a new way of life, because men were discovering a new personal contact with God.

The practical application of this quickened conscience did not appear at once. Though Wesley himself tried endless experiments by way of object lessons, their full flowering was postponed or overshadowed by contemporary conditions. He pleaded for prison reform, for the abolition of slavery and for the right use of wealth. He attempted local schemes to relieve unemployment by throwing open his church premises and providing yarn so that poor women might weave and earn an honest livelihood. He subsidized small tradesmen hard hit by contemporary circumstances. He established schools and orphanages, and opened dispensaries for the poor. In countless ways he strove to apply the teaching of Christ to everyday life and work. If one is to estimate the outcome of these experiments one must look at England a hundred years after. The tedious and cruel drain of the long war with France, the corrupt political system which made mockery of the franchise and shut out the people from any share in legislation, and the sudden changes wrought by the industrial revolution, delayed the issue. In 1832, after the Reform Bill was passed, there began a long sequence of humanitarian acts and philanthropic enterprises which may be traced to their origin in the eighteenth-century revival of religion.

It is true, therefore, to say that Wesley, by the grace of God, changed England. The revolution was seen immediately in the lives of countless individuals and subsequently in the whole moral and spiritual life and conduct of the nation.

Whilst he and his itinerant preachers travelled the land, from north to south and east to west, the people who were impressed and 'converted' by their preaching made very few journeys. The mobility of labour was not yet achieved. The little groups or societies needed constant oversight and there was no settled ministry. The tiny communities had lay leaders, and since the organization, such as it was, maintained the characteristics of a family, the leader's oversight was paternal. These loosely defined fellowships assumed the form of class-meetings in 1742. There was still a debt on the property at Bristol. One of the members, Captain Foy, suggested a solution to the financial problem. 'Let every member of the society give a penny a week, till the debt is paid,' he said. In answer to an objection that some were too poor to make even that modest contribution, he replied, 'Then put eleven of the poorest with me; and if they can give anything, well; I will call on them weekly; and if they can give nothing, I will give for them as well as for myself. And each of you call on eleven ot your neighbours weekly; receive what they give, and make up what is wanting'.

The plan succeeded, and developed a pastorate which was much more important in its spiritual contacts than in its financial results. In some ways it became a pattern for the democratic movements of the next century.

The early Christian Church had issued symbols of membership called tesserae, and, on similar lines, tickets were devised for the members of these class-meetings. As the numbers increased the leaders met together, and their meeting became the court of discipline. Every three months each class was visited by an itinerant preacher – Wesley or one of his helpers – and the quarterly tickets were renewed. By such simple methods the whole of the people were linked up, the moral and spiritual levels were maintained by the exclusion of those who had 'fallen from grace', and a brotherhood of believers created all over England long before there was any question of establishing a separate Church. The Societies, considered as a whole, made up 'the people called Methodists'.

Such a sense of family and of common kinship was unique in eighteenth-century England. It challenged class distinctions, and united rich and poor, educated and illiterate, in a way quite new. Since it was founded on a spiritual experience, it began to express itself in corporate acts of Christian service which gradually permeated and helped to change the whole community. From the beginning the revival was founded on individual experience. Every year made it more evident that personal salvation must precede social redemption. The lives of thousands of the early Methodists confirm this as a vital principle.

Many of the men whom Wesley influenced directly, left all to become preachers of the gospel. They furnish a body of evidence which is invaluable. Amongst them was a Yorkshire stonemason born in Birstal in 1707. 'John Nelson', said Southey, 'had as high a spirit, and as brave a heart, as ever Englishman was blessed with.' As a boy he had been introspective. Going to London to follow his trade his mind was restless and dissatisfied. None of the preachers he heard solved his problems. 'Even George Whitefield', he said, 'was to me as a man who could play well on an instrument; for his preaching was pleasant to me and I loved the man; so that if any one offered to disturb him, I was ready to fight for him. But I did not understand him, though I might hear him twenty times for ought I know.'

In this mood of uncertainty he struggled on, playing his obscure part in building the French Church in Spitalfields. He was just one of a gang of labourers in a London street. Then something happened.

On Sunday, June 17, 1739, he found himself standing in a crowd gathered at 6.45 a.m. on Moorfields to hear John Wesley preach. He was fairly near the front – was he not a Yorkshireman? At first he was just one amongst seven thousand others, then he was isolated – a solitary soul facing his destiny!

The crowd stirred a little as the preacher moved through the midst. 'As soon as he got upon the stand, he stroked back his hair and turned his face towards where I stood, and I thought fixed his eyes upon me. His countenance struck such an awful dread upon me before I heard him speak, but it made my heart beat like the pendulum of a clock; and when he did speak, I said, "This man can tell the secrets of my heart; he hath not left me there; for he hath the remedy, even the blood of Jesus".'

In that hour he made his choice. His defences were down. He welcomed his Lord. Such a sense of individual challenge was constantly experienced by people who heard John Wesley – even when they were lost in a huge crowd. The message and the messenger isolated them, and left them face to face with Jesus.

Back to his work he went, his convictions strengthened but his task unchanged. All through the winter he lived sparingly, fasting from Thursday night to Saturday morning and giving away the food he would otherwise have eaten. It was a rough and ready test of the reality of his experience.

Going one day to St. Paul's Cathedral for Holy Communion he felt God strangely near. Kneeling in the shadows he cried out softly, 'Thy will be done,

Thy will be done'. Some inner voice seemed to be commanding him to return to Yorkshire. He argued against it but he could not long resist. His pitiful little bundle was packed and he set out. At Birstal he was discouraged. His friends thought him mad. His mother said, 'Your head is turned'. He answered, 'Yes, and my heart too'. The neighbours talked – his wife was ashamed. He preached to them all, until wife, mother, neighbours knelt with him at the Saviour's feet.

He began to preach in the district. The clergy and ministers tried to restrain him as a fanatic. He fell on his knees and prayed aloud, 'I am not my own, but Thine; therefore, Thy will be done in me, on me, and by me'. As he rose it seemed that the clouds broke and light was everywhere.

Little knots of people gathered to hear him. He would come straight from work, his leather apron fastened with a piece of rope through which was stuck his hammer and trowel. Mounting a stand, he would hitch up the clumsy apron and begin to preach – a John the Baptist proclaiming repentance and hope. Mobs threatened and ill used him, but nothing silenced him. Every hour that he served his Lord made him more sure, more determined, more courageous.

At last a great day dawned. John Wesley sent for him to go to London. His wife looked out his clothes – they were very worn. He looked at her tenderly and said, 'I have worn them out in the Lord's work, and He will not let me want long'. Just before he started on his journey some one brought him a piece of blue cloth for a coat, and some black cloth for waistcoat and breeches. 'The Lord is mindful of them that trust in Him,' he cried, and set out for London.

He did not stay long there, for Wesley desired him to go westward to Oxford, to Bristol and to Cornwall. Sometimes he shared a horse with another preacher. For several weeks he slept on bare boards, rolling up his great-coat to serve as pillow for John Wesley, and resting his own head on Burkitt's *Notes on the New Testament*! In the middle of a sleepless night John turned over for the hundredth time and exclaimed, 'Brother Nelson, let us be of good cheer. I have one whole side yet, for the skin is off but on one side'.

Food was scarce, and in these earlier days hospitality was not readily offered. Wesley accepted the conditions philosophically and his companions learnt from him. 'Brother Nelson,' he said as they tightened their belts, 'we ought to be thankful that there are plenty of blackberries, for this is the best country I ever saw for getting a stomach, but the worst that ever I saw for getting food.' Sometimes a cottager took them into his house, dried their clothes and gave them a meal. In the dimly lit room they would kneel and pray together, and know that One stood in their midst, risen triumphant Son of God. Amazing love, how could it be! As they knelt there they knew it to be true. As they took their leave they rejoiced for another heart strangely warmed. So the flame spread.

The converts were not the product of a momentary emotion. They stood the test of hardship and persecution unflinching. Materially they lost many things; spiritually they gained all. In Leeds Mrs. Nelson was ill-treated by the mob. They beat her and killed her child. She did not waver in her faith. When her husband returned he took up his work, once more, toiling as a stonemason from five in the morning till six at night, and then going out, in the evening, to preach.

A plot was devised by some of the local clergy and innkeepers. They must get rid of the pestilent rogue who presumed to be a preacher. They would have him 'pressed for a soldier'. His neighbours warned him, but he was not afraid. At Pudsey the constables waited for him. He rode to the inn to talk to them. They were nonplussed. How could they take him? He was not a vagrant. For a few days more he went unmolested. At Adwalton, immediately he finished preaching, the constable's deputy, an innkeeper, arrested him. He must join the Army. By whose orders? The townsmen and the clergy demanded it. Ten hours later the warrant came. At Birstal the commissioners were amused. 'Why have you brought this man?' they said. 'Because the people don't like so much preaching,' the constable answered sheepishly. The magistrates laughed, and one, swearing lustily, declared the man should be a soldier and have preaching enough. 'Sir, you are not to swear,' said John. 'You have no right to preach,' bellowed the man suddenly angry. 'Sir,' said John very calmly, 'I have as much right to preach as you have to swear.' There was nothing to do with such a cool customer but to commit him to the guard. He was marched off to Halifax, and presently to Bradford.

Underneath a slaughter-house, in a vile little cell three feet square, he was thrown with another 'pressed' man. There was no room to sit. He crouched on the floor – happily! 'My soul was so filled with the love of God that it was Paradise to me.' Darkness fell. Now, if the comfortable critics who talk glibly of neurotics and poseurs be right, we shall find him dejected and collapsed. The prisoner hears the sound of footsteps. Food and water are pushed through the hole in the door. Candles follow. John Nelson gives God thanks. His friends will surely bid him good night and go to their beds. That is not the reaction of warmed hearts! All through the hours of darkness they stay outside the grim little door, below the slaughter-house. They are singing hymns of joy and faith. There is no morbid sympathizing. It would be absurd. Inside the noisome little cell the

162

stonemason is singing as cheerfully as they. 'Sir,' says his fellow prisoner, astonished, 'are all these your kinsfolk that they love you so well?' John answers happily, 'By this you may know that they are Jesus Christ's disciples'. It was this new sense of kinship with God Himself which revolutionized the life of thousands.

So he became a soldier, and the regiment marched on to York. People lined the streets to see him! The officers forbade him to preach, but in giving him his orders they swore roundly. This gave John the text and the occasion for a sermon! He reproved them for their bad language. They brought him a gun. 'I will bear it as a cross,' he said. They marched him to Heworth Moor to drill, but the corporal bade him lay down the gun and talk to him about God. The people were curious, and followed him through the streets when he was off duty. They begged him to preach to them on Sunday morning. He told them he would 'take a walk on to the moor at half an hour after seven'. To the moor he went, and there found three hundred people waiting to hear him. At night he preached in several houses. On Monday his officers threatened him with a flogging if he dared to preach again, but crowds followed him everywhere – not to hustle him but to listen to his words. He was thrown into the guardroom and later brought before the Major, who listened to the charges against him. 'Well, if that be all, it is no crime,' said he. 'When you have done your duty I do not care if you preach every night in a house or any private place out of the town, but I would not have you make any mobs. Go back to your quarters, and if there is some convenient time I will hear you preach myself, for I wish all men were like you.'

Northwards to Easingwold, on to Northallerton and Durham the regiment marched. At every opportunity John preached and never lacked an audience. Suddenly he was discharged, through the influence of the Earl of Stair, a friend of the Countess of Huntingdon. The Major sent for him. 'I wish you well wherever you go,' he said, 'for I believe you Methodists are a well-meaning people.' There was a murmur of assent from the other officers. John gave them each a little book and took his leave. Back in the barracks his comrades crowded round him. 'We are glad you are free,' they said, 'but sorry to let you go.' Here again is a difficult problem for the superficial critic who finds that Wesley and his preachers drove men mad and did more harm than good. The neurotic and introspective stonemason had been changed completely. He was certainly an embarrassment to a regiment! Why should his officers give him a kindly farewell? Why should his comrades regret his going, yet rejoice in his good fortune on being discharged? It is a unanimous verdict from a surprising jury. One does not associate a regimental mess or a barrack-room with sentimentality or flattery. John Nelson was a man – a man, moreover, who told them of the certainties of God.

All over the kingdom similar changes were taking place in individuals. Contemporary literature affords a mass of irrefutable evidence. It is not the record of passing emotions but the account of lives permanently changed; the hopeless suddenly accepted a goal and bent all their energies towards reaching it; the arrogant and selfish saw the sorrows of their neighbours and forgot all else save that they might serve them; the gross and sensual learnt new spiritual values, because they had entered into a new spiritual relationship.

There was John Murlin, cursing, drunken miserable Cornish farmer, to whom came 'a great deliverance'. Very reluctantly he became leader of 'a little class', and buying 'a large Bible with other books', found himself saying presently, 'it pleased God to open my understanding more and more'.

There was John Lancaster, backslider, who stole candlesticks and velvet and was condemned to death. In Newgate, Sarah Peters, the ministering angel who gave her life to the comforting of condemned felons, led him back again to life and hope. He was not reprieved by man but he was pardoned by God! That last night, with five others in the condemned cell, he prayed not for himself but for the salvation of the world! As the grim cart rumbled along through the crowd to the place where the gallows stood, he cried out, like John the Baptist, that they should repent. Then he burst into song, the song which Charles Wesley had written for such an occasion.

> Think on us, who think on Thee,
>   And every struggling soul release!
> O remember Calvary
>   And bid us go in peace.

His corpse was taken from the gibbet by men, hired by surgeons who hoped it might be used for experiments, but a crowd of sailors chased them, and securing the poor lifeless body carried it tenderly to his mother that she might bury it decently. Why should the sailors bother? Why should old Sarah Peters spend her life in those tragic cells?

Charity children become respectable citizens, old folk lost to decency and longing to die become young in spirit and joyous in service, soldiers sunk in brutality learn a new meaning in sacrifice – England is changing because individuals are being changed. It is not the dilettanti, sitting in the coffee-houses, sipping their wine and reading the *Spectator*, who accomplish the transformation by their pretty wit; it is rather the ordinary people out in the fields preaching, or busied with commonplace tasks singing the new song at their work – these wayfaring men transfigured by a new experience. They are no longer inarticulate, indefinite parts of a mass; they have acquired a new individuality, a new sense of the supernatural, a new vision of the Kingdom of God. Hell may be real but Heaven is very near. Their words may be grotesque at times, but their lives are being lifted out of the gutter to heights of sacrificial service that are sublime. They cannot contain the good news. They spread it everywhere. To Scotland, Ireland, and Wales the Wesleys go, and little groups of people become the nucleus of bigger Societies.

Ignorant men became cultured and scholarly. The son of a village carpenter – Thomas Walsh – became the best Biblical scholar Wesley ever knew. Speaking only Erse, he taught himself Hebrew and Greek, so that 'he could tell you, after a pause, how often any word occurred in the Bible, where it was found and what its particular meaning was in any given context'. Listen to his prayer as he began his studies, each day: 'Lord Jesus, I lay my soul at Thy feet to be taught and governed by Thee. Take the veil from the mystery, and show me the truth as it is in Thyself. Be Thou my sun and star by day and by night.'

More than forty times John Wesley crossed the Irish Sea, nursing the little Societies in their most difficult circumstances. He took fourteen journeys to Scotland, and preached at Edinburgh to crowds of twenty thousand people. In America the work spread, because three people came with transfigured souls – Barbara Heck, Philip Embury the carpenter, and Captain Webb the soldier.

It is absurd to say that the revival was temporary either in its influence on individuals or on the English nation. Its ethical results were seen in the growth of Sunday schools, the better moral tone of the Army, the Universities, the purification of literature, the increasing amenities of hospitals, the reform of Poor Relief, the decrease of crime, the more humane and reformative method of penal procedure, and the gradual lessening of political corruption. These movements, and many like them, were not suddenly and finally effective. The progress of the next two centuries was influenced by the spiritual forces which began to be harnessed by the Wesleys and their comrades.

The words of Professor Rufus Jones, the distinguished Quaker philosopher, summarize the position with great clarity:

'One of the most dynamic things the modern world has seen was that same evangelical movement in the days when it *moved*, with its original high *caloric*. It came like a vernal equinox into the morally dull and static life of the eighteenth century. It turned water to wine, it brought prodigals home, it raised life out of death. It produced miracles of transformation. But the most remarkable thing about it was the freshly inspired social impulse which it produced. It reformed prisons, it stopped the slave trade, it freed slaves. It made its converts uncomfortable over wrong social conditions. It sent missionaries to create hospitals and to conquer ignorance in almost every land on the globe. It was always as much outward as it was inward, though its creative spring was assuredly a birth of new life from the central Source of Life.'

CHAPTER II

HE DID NOT GROW OLD

TIME laid his hand gently on John Wesley. The years were more crammed with activities than before, but he showed no diminished energies. To-day the Charterhouse School Song reminds us again of a man who never grew old.

> Wesley, John Wesley, was one of our company,
> Prophet untiring and fearless of tongue;
> Down the long years he went
> Spending, yet never spent,
> Serving his God with a heart ever young.

Towards the end of his long life he maintained a vigorous and unwearied appearance, according to a description of one of his preachers, John Hampson. 'The figure of Mr. Wesley was remarkable. His stature was of the lowest, his habit of body in every period of life the reverse of corpulent, and expressive of strict temperance and continual exercise; and, notwithstanding his small size, his step was firm, and his appearance, till within a few years of his death, vigorous and muscular. His face, for an old man, was one of the finest we have seen. A clear, smooth forehead, an aquiline nose, an eye the brightest and the most piercing that can be conceived, and a freshness of complexion scarcely ever to be found at his years, and impressive of the most perfect health, conspired to render him a venerable and interesting figure. Few have seen him without being struck with his appearance; and many, who have been greatly prejudiced against him, have been known to change their opinion the moment they were introduced into his presence. In his countenance and demeanour there was a cheerfulness mingled with gravity; a sprightliness which was the natural result of an unusual flow of spirits, and was yet accompanied with every mark of the most serene tranquillity. His aspect, particularly in profile, had a strong character of acuteness and penetration. In dress he was a pattern of neatness and simplicity. A narrow, plaited stock, a coat with small upright collar, no buckles at the knees, no silk or velvet in any part of his apparel, and a head as white as snow, gave an idea of something primitive and apostolical; while an air of neatness and cleanliness was diffused over his whole person.'

None of his contemporaries faced more problems than he, and none concentrated on their solution so remorselessly. He had to defend himself and his Societies against attacks by the clergy and laity, in sermons, speeches, periodicals, and tracts. He had to devise and control the gradually evolving administrative machinery of what was becoming a Church, though he was unwilling to recognize the fact. Conferences of preachers, disciplinary courts of the leaders, and the co-ordination of all the little Societies must be developed and guided. Though it was inevitable that he should assume autocratic powers that almost amounted to benevolent dictatorship, it was equally necessary that he should prepare his successors for the day when he should be no more in their midst. As Methodism grew, more rapidly than he realized, a new problem as to the actual ownership of its property was created. In 1784 there were 359 Methodist chapels in the United Kingdom. On February 28, he executed the Deed of Declaration or Model Deed which appointed a hundred preachers as legally constituting the Conference. This body had a legal and continuous existence, held the chapels in trust and appointed ministers. It might have created a kind of 'upper house' amongst the Methodist ministry, but it remained until its dissolution in 1932, merely the instrument which confirmed the actions of the whole Conference, making them valid in the eyes of the law.

One other major problem had been created by the spread of Methodism overseas. When the American Colonies established their Independence most of the Methodist preachers serving there returned to England. There was no longer an ordained clergyman amongst those left. All the non-Methodist Anglicans had left America as soon as war broke out. The colonists began to complain that their ministers were not authorized to administer the Sacraments. They would gladly have agreed to their taking upon themselves the necessary powers. John Wesley was shocked by the thought of such irregularity. The Bishop of London refused to help him by ordaining one of the Methodist preachers who was leaving for America.

At this crisis he decided to send out Dr. Thomas Coke, himself in Anglican Orders, to superintend the work. He refused to go unless he received authority from Wesley to act virtually as bishop. 'The more maturely I consider the matter, the more expedient it appears to me that the power of ordaining others should be received by me from you, by imposition of your hand.' So wrote Dr. Coke and John Wesley was convinced that the time had come for him to take the drastic step. On September 10, 1784, relying on his belief that as presbyter of the Church of England he possessed the adequate authority, he ordained Dr. Coke as Superintendent, and Whatcoat and Vasey as presbyters, to serve in America. The die was cast.

As real necessity arose he proceeded to ordain preachers for work in Scotland, in Ireland and the West Indies. His brother Charles was shocked beyond measure. He wrote to Dr. Chandler, 'I can scarcely yet believe it, that in his eighty-second year, my brother, my old intimate friend and companion, should have assumed the episcopal character, ordained elders, consecrated a bishop, and sent him to ordain our lay preachers in America. . . . Lord Mansfield told me last year that ordination was separation. This my brother does not and will not see; or that he has renounced the principles and practice of his whole life'. But John remained adamant. He was convinced that he had acted within his rights as a presbyter, and Charles, though disagreeing, remained loyal and affectionate. The actual separation of Methodism from the Church of England did not take place till both the brothers were dead.

In spite of these intricate and vital problems, and in spite of his continual journeyings from one end of the kingdom to the other, John Wesley remained young in spirit and unimpaired in health.

In 1764 when he was sixty-two years old, he breakfasted with George Whitefield, 'who seemed to be an old, old man, being fairly worn out in his Master's service, though he has hardly seen fifty years'. In himself John Wesley felt 'no difference from what I was at five-and-twenty, only that I have fewer teeth, and more grey hairs'.

At seventy-two he declared that his sight was better and his nerves stronger than they were thirty years before. What was the secret of his youthfulness? That was a question he sometimes asked himself, and answered: 'The chief means are – 1. My constantly rising at four for about fifty years. 2. My generally preaching at five in the morning; one of the most healthy exercises in the world. 3. My never travelling less, by sea and land, than four thousand five hundred miles in a year.'

At seventy-eight he rejoiced that he had preached three times a day for seven days.

On September 25, 1785, he made a somewhat apologetic entry in his *Journal*, 'I now applied myself in earnest to the writing of Mr. Fletcher's Life, having procured the best materials I could. To this I dedicated all the time I could spare till November, from five in the morning till eight at night. These are my studying hours. I can not write any longer in a day without hurting my eyes'. That same year, when he was eighty-three years old, he travelled seventy-six miles in a day and preached three times, remarking, 'I was no more tired than when I rose in the morning'.

At eighty-seven years of age he wrote on March 26, 1790, 'I finished my sermon on the Wedding Garment; perhaps the last I shall write. My eyes are now waxed dim; my natural force is abated. However, while I can, I would fain do a little for God before I drop in the dust. . . . In the evening I preached to a crowded audience at Salop'. So it goes on, without a single trace of morbid apprehension or any desire to slow down. In May he was up in Scotland. 'We returned to Aberdeen, and I took a solemn farewell of a crowded audience. If I should be permitted to see them again, well; if not, I have delivered my own soul.'

There are those who still imagine him to have been

solemn, almost inhuman, in his detachment from the
joys of life. This is completely untrue. Few men
loved the freedom of the open road better than he,
few were more observant of its passing interests.
He would constantly turn aside to see a famous
building or to visit some historic spot. As he rode
he read, yet was never too absorbed in his book to
talk with other travellers. Nor was he so sourly
intolerant of other people's amusements as some have
suggested. He had his own opinions and stated them
fairly and, on the whole, with tolerance. As a schoolboy he saw *Macbeth* and on several occasions went to
Latin plays given by the boys of Westminster.
Occasionally he listened to an oratorio though not
without feeling he must make certain caustic comments. 'There are two things in all modern pieces of
music which I could never reconcile to common
sense: One is, singing the same words ten times over;
the other, singing different words by different
persons, at one and the same time.'

Sometimes he went to concerts given by his
nephews, the sons of Charles Wesley. It is evident
that he was less narrow than some of his contemporaries. 'John Wesley, in gown and bands, attended
one of the concerts with his wife, to show that he did
not consider that there was any sin in such entertain-
ments, as some of the Methodists were inclined to
think.'

On February 10, 1787, he wrote: 'At six I preached

on Hebrews iv. 14. In the afternoon I went with a gentleman to hear the famous musician that plays upon the glasses. By my appearing there (as I had foreseen) a heap of gentry attended in the evening; and I believe several of them, as well as Mr. T. himself, did not come in vain.' There is a sane humanity in the man who could, quite conscientiously, go to the entertainment between his two services on Friday.

At eighty-five years of age he visited 'the celebrated wax-works at the museum in Spring Gardens', and in the evening of the same day preached at Peckham 'to a more awakened congregation than ever I observed there before'. Evidently the morning 'dissipation' had not affected his ability to hold and to arouse his hearers.

There was a richer humanity in his make-up than some people have realized, yet it was a humanity which never lost its proper sense of relative values. His youthful spirit survived the onslaught of the years because within his heart was a peace the world could neither give nor take away. Deep down, beyond the reach of all contrary winds or sudden gales, was the untroubled calm which comes from infinite resources – the tranquillity of one who knows he can rely upon the inexhaustible love of God.

All through the long years he had been blessed with friends. His own vibrant personality attracted men and women and little children to him for very joy of his companionship. He could have been the

centre of a circle which would have made the
Johnsonian group look small and tawdry by comparison, but he possessed what Dr. Johnson could not
understand, a sense of purpose, of urgency, and of
eternal values. 'I hate to meet John Wesley', said
Johnson petulantly to Boswell; 'the dog enchants me
with his conversation, and then breaks away to go
and visit some old woman.' It was impossible for
the old oracle of Fleet Street to realize that a man
might feel an inward compulsion to render strict
account of every hour he lived. How could he know,
as he sat comfortably on his favourite settle, that the
little man, whose brilliant mind so matched his own,
was urged from his retreat to be off about his Master's
business? 'He is never at leisure', he said almost wistfully. Perhaps the old doctor heard so many other
voices that he did not hear the Voice which called
his friend away. If there had been just a dash of
Johnson in Wesley, and the 'warmed heart' in
Johnson what a team they would have made!

His friends were many, his admirers innumerable
and his lovers – perhaps fewer than some of his
biographers have imagined! His personal contacts,
especially with women, were child-like and ingenu-
ous. There were a few people who shared a deeper
intimacy. It is difficult to judge how far they
influenced his career or how long they remained
active forces in his life. His chief concern was his
vocation as a preacher of the gospel. Even a casual

glance at the record of that work in the *Dictionary of National Biography*, in his *Journal*, or in any serious study of his life, will make that fact clear.

Unfortunately, few of the women, whose associations with him have been described in such highly coloured language, were able to enter deeply into his religious struggle or to appreciate the urgency of his evangelism. For a moment they seemed to make a sudden appeal, and then to fade away like ghosts, frightened by his austerity, repelled by his methodical routine or just left astonished at one whose gentleness had charmed them but whose busyness made him forget their existence. So Sally Kirkham, Mrs. Pendarves, and Sophie Hopkey cross his path, and make him stop a moment happily, but the moment passes and he rides on. From Oxford to America, from Georgia to England and the 'work of the Lord' – it must have been more puzzling to them than disturbing to him. He did not leave behind him a trail of broken hearts, nor did he ride on deeply wounded himself. He was so passionate a crusader that such contacts were of secondary importance. His honour and his heart remained intact.

The real love story of John Wesley is almost modern in its heavy sense of tragedy, and its vague unhappy ending. It has been brilliantly told in a short study by Mrs. Elsie Harrison. None of the longer books are more than chronicles of events, but her words throb with the anguish of heart-breaking days John Wesley spent with Grace Murray. From that experience he did not emerge heart-whole. Perhaps it was necessary that he should pass through such fires. In mind and body he came out unscorched but his soul had known the torment of unjust, unnecessary frustration. When he rode across the hills a happy lover, eager to keep the promised tryst, he found his dream shattered. She had married John Bennet, the ambitious, rebellious Methodist preacher. Condemn Charles for his interference, or Grace for her mistaken judgement, but John Wesley stands out a tragic figure, stripped of the great love of his life. The desire of his eyes, as he put it, was taken from him with a stroke. It was more even than that. Humanly speaking Grace Murray remained for Wesley, the desire of his heart. The lovers were separated. Grace went to take up a strange but faithful task as consort to a stormy petrel. John, forty-four years of age, passed through a valley of deep shadows, squared his shoulders and came out to do battle for the Lord again. Grace looked far beyond even the future towards a timeless joy, and unearthly fellowship which should be granted to her hungry heart. For her came consolation in the children she bore. John rode on alone, even though he married Mrs. Vazeille. He was incapable of sharing quiet or unquiet domesticity. It would be difficult to blame his unfortunate wife for all the broken record of their marriage. The only marriage he could have transfigured was one which would have given him a comrade at his side, riding the roads of England with the message of his Lord. Such a comrade Grace Murray might have been. Their ways divided but the human factors in the tragedy are beyond our judgement. Charles Wesley, John Bennet, and some others assumed the right of guidance which God alone may exercise or delegate. Grace Murray and John Wesley went their separate ways, accepting the pitiful facts and remembering the divine opportunity. In all England there was no messenger of God more blithe in his proclamation of the Good News than John Wesley; in all England there was no man whose heart bore deeper wound.

The years brought their new challenge, and stored up the memories that bless and burn. He heard the challenge, and tucked away the memories for some convenient season when his work should be done. He had no time for the luxury of morbid recollection. Men waited for the message – God's message through him. He mounted his horse and rode on, till the toll of the years grew heavy. Reluctantly he took to a chaise, and rattled over the rough roads reading hard between the stopping-places. The little bookshelf he had fixed in the ungainly carriage carried comrades no one could take away.

His earthly friends were translated one by one. Vincent Perronet and John Fletcher passed on, leaving him the lonelier. His brother Charles began to fail,

In January and February 1788, John wrote to him several times. He was insistent that his brother should go out each day. He begged him not to spare expense. 'I can make that up. You shall not die to save charges.' He sent prescriptions to his brother's wife. Time could not be stayed and Charles Wesley died on March 29, 1788. John did not hear the news for five days. He was preaching at Madeley and Salop, at Stafford and Burslem, at Newcastle-under-Lyme, and Leek. Meanwhile his brother was buried in Marylebone Churchyard in ground 'as holy as any in England', as John wrote when he heard. 'It contains a large quantity of "bonny dust".' On April 4 he drove through a violent storm to Macclesfield, and there received the letter telling him Charles was dead. There is no reference in his *Journal* or his *Diary*. He could not write glibly of such things.

He cannot stop, even now, to mourn. On from Macclesfield to Bullock Smithy, to Ashton, Oldham, Northwich, Warrington, Liverpool, Wigan, and Bolton. It is only a fortnight since he heard the news of Charles's death. The crowded congregation sings well. They bow in prayer. Again it is time to sing. The tired hands turn the leaves of the book. He has found the place:

> Come, O Thou Traveller unknown,
> Whom still I hold, but cannot see!
> My company before is gone,
> And I am left alone with Thee . . .

He cannot end the verse. The pent-up tears have burst the dam. He sinks down on the pulpit seat, burying his face in his hands. There is a deep hush everywhere – deepest in his own heart. Charles is rushing in to that tidy room at Lincoln College, scattering the papers left and right, Susanna is teaching him his alphabet in Epworth, old Samuel is giving him the precious book on Job – 'gone, and I am left alone . . . with Thee'. He brushes away the last tear, stands up and sings,

> What though my shrinking flesh complain,
>   And murmur to contend so long?
> I rise superior to my pain,
>   When I am weak, then I am strong . . .

It is Charles's hymn, and the people are singing it now like 'the singing of angels in our Father's house'. The moment of anguish is passed. Wrestling Jacob is on his feet again.

> Through all eternity to prove
> Thy nature and Thy name is Love.

Yet a year or two more he rides through England and Wales preaching to sinners and strengthening those who struggled to be saints.

In February 1791, his plans for his next journey were nearly complete. He would preach through England again. But he had made a mistake. It was a longer journey he must take. One last entry in his

Diary – the *Journal* ended on October 24, 1790. At 4.45 a.m. he was at prayer, and the last word for the day was '9.30 prayed'. One more sermon to be preached – at Leatherhead on February 23, 1791. One more letter to be written – to Wilberforce, protesting against 'that execrable villainy' the slave trade, urging him to continue in his struggle to abolish it. 'Go on, in the name of God and in the power of His might, till even American slavery (the vilest that ever saw the sun) shall vanish away before it.'

His work is almost done. He is back in his room at City Road. There are signs that a new and longer journey is impending. He need not pack his belongings. The little book-shelf in the chaise is empty; the two silver spoons are safe; the little Bible is in good keeping. Friends come to see him in those days that linger a little. Once he sings and his voice is quite strong.

> I'll praise my Maker while I've breath
> And when my voice is lost in death,
> Praise shall employ my nobler powers;
> My days of praise shall ne'er be past,
> While life, and thought, and being last,
> Or immortality endures.

Or immortality endures! Here is proof it is unending. Those eighty-seven years point to something beyond the range of time. They are but madness if they end in death.

The weary wheels of life are turning very slowly

now. His brother's wife stoops over him. He whispers faintly, 'He giveth His beloved rest'. The wheels turn slower still. He cries out one last triumphant certainty, 'The best of all is God is with us', and again, 'Farewell'.

The wheels have stopped. The horse he rode is forgotten. The old chaise stands empty. The weary wheels at last stand still. He does not need them. His soul is winged. The wings are spread. He is away.

Printed in Great Britain by
The Camelot Press Ltd., London and Southampton